Somalis

IN MINNESOTA

Ahmed Ismail Yusuf

**Minnesota Historical
Society Press**

To the memory of my great friend and mentor,
Professor Fred Pfeil of Trinity College, Hartford, Connecticut

www.mhspress.org

The Minnesota Historical Society Press is a member of the Association of American University Presses.

Manufactured in the United States of America

10 9 8 7 6 5 4 3 2 1

♾ The paper used in this publication meets the minimum requirements of the American National Standard for Information Sciences—Permanence for Printed Library Materials, ANSI Z39.48–1984.

International Standard Book Number
ISBN: 978-0-87351-867-3 (paper)
ISBN: 978-0-87351-874-1 (e-book)

Library of Congress Cataloging-in-Publication Data

Yusuf, Ahmed Ismail.
    Somalis in Minnesota / Ahmed Ismail Yusuf.
      p. cm. — (The People of Minnesota)
    Includes bibliographical references and index.
    ISBN 978-0-87351-867-3 (pbk. : alk. paper) — ISBN 978-0-87351-874-1 (ebook)
        1. Somalis—Minnesota. 2. Somali Americans—Minnesota. I. Title.
F615.S67Y87   2013
977.600493′54—dc23
                                                                          2012037508

This and other Minnesota Historical Society Press books are available from popular e-book vendors.

Front cover: Photo by David McGrath, courtesy TVbyGIRLS
Back cover: Photo by Bill Jolitz

Cover design by Running Rhino Design.
Book design and composition by Wendy Holdman.

Contents

Map of Somalia

Somalis

IN MINNESOTA

A fever of flag fashion: many Somalis celebrate Somali Independence Day by wearing all blue, the color of the Somali flag with its five-pointed white star.

Prologue

S OMALIS WOULD TRUST THREE WORDS in their language to tell a tale about them: *sahan, war,* and *martisoor.* These three words define certain economic, social, and cultural behaviors that would fit most Somalis, particularly those from the north, who have nomadic traditions. Even southern Somalis, with their more sedentary lifestyles of farming and urbanization, would agree that these words carry an enormous weight in describing a Somali's historical, anecdotal identity. Consequently, these three words are the thread to understanding how Somalis flocked to Minnesota.

Sahan: The closest meaning in English is "pioneer." *Sahan* burdens itself with the daunting danger of the unknown: "to be the first to open or prepare a way for settlement." The Somali person entrusted with *sahan* is normally a male who is solely in charge of judging, weighing, and weeding out all hazards seen or heard during his journey. He is expected to appraise the quantity of grazing grass and water available on the land he is exploring and to know how far away it is from the previous home. He also must investigate what types of predators would share the habitat and identify the potential enemies that threaten. The *sahan* must have already assessed, sorted, and evaluated all risks against the ultimate economic advantage when he brings or sends back *war* (news) to the clan, endorsing the relocation of a whole community to the new land.

War: Somalis are known to be loquacious, and word of mouth travels with mighty speed on a news mill called *war. War,* in literal translation as a noun, is "news." When it is an adjective, however, it takes on multiple meanings: *war, waryaa, warran, warrama, warkeen, warkaa, warsan, warraysi, warrayso, waraysteen, waraystay, waraystay* (news, People of News, give the news, tell us the news, he or she who brought in the news, what news?, good news, news inquiry, ask for news, they asked for news, he asked for news, she asked for news). Additionally, Somalis are known as the *Waryaa Sayers,* which in loose English translation means "People of News." Somalis call out *waryaa,* implying "you, who are the news carrier, come and share it," to get someone's attention. *War* and *warraysi* (news and gathering news) are woven into their cultural existence. A nomad, for example, would pass on the *war* to another, in inquiry (*warraysi*) form. Urban-dwelling Somalis always gather around TVs and radios as though there is twenty-four-hour "breaking news." Thus, a male on *sahan* would stop any potential news carrier he sees along the path, asking "*warran*/give the news up." Once the other tells him all he knows, the *sahan* in return would retell all he has learned through his travels and previous life.

Martisoor: Throughout his travel time, the *sahan,* who is on foot, does not carry a supply of food and water with him, for he has to make himself as light as possible. He thus must live off the *martisoor* (hospitality) and generosity of strangers. He will not perish from thirst or starvation because of the Somalis' unwavering custom of graceful hospitality. Even the name *Soomaali,* consisting of two words, *soo* and *maal,* means "Go and milk it for yourself," or, more loosely, "Help yourself to the milk." The traditional definition states that a traveler came upon a Somali family with a lactating cow, and the father, the patriarch, told the guest, "Go milk the cow for yourself." Thus was born the name *Soomaal,* which later evolved into *Soomaali.* The *sahan* is provided with temporary shelter and fed throughout the journey. Traditionally, he is also safe from assault of any kind. Anyone who inflicts the slightest infraction on a *sahan* or traveling guest would bear grave social disdain.

The symbiotic relationship between the *sahan* and *war* has been in place for ages as the Somali camel herders traveling throughout the land learned about impending dangers, seasonal changes, and world happenings from fellow travelers.

Consequently, when *war* about jobs drifted from Minnesota, a few came on *sahan* to authenticate it, and many followed. Encountering *martisoor* in Minnesota, they found their house of hope and began to tell, all by word of mouth that rippled through the Somali *war* grapevine: there are jobs in Minnesota, and hospitality is found there as well.

Somalis in Minnesota

In the early 1990s, many Minnesota citizens noticed a trickle of conspicuously dressed Africans, especially women in colorful attire, some veiled and some with simple head-scarves, arriving at schools, grocery stores, supermarkets, and shopping centers, sharing both resources and space. As their numbers began to grow, questions about them arose: Who are these people? Where are they from? To what religious faith do they belong?

The basic answers came quickly. They are from an East African tropical nation called Somalia, the people are called Somalis, their language is Somali, and their distinctive women's attire is in accordance with their faith, Islam. Then new questions replaced the old: What was their past like? What brought them to the United States? Why did Somalis choose Minnesota, an icy, arctic-like state with its acclimatized Scandinavian and German populations? These three questions, in various tones, have persisted tenaciously. This book will attempt to answer them, briefly touching on Somalis' cultural affiliation, economic aspirations, political participation, religious faith, and educational opportunities.

As this poem (song) illustrates, few Somalis, before they lost all they had known, would leave their families for longer than required to earn a livelihood in Europe or the Middle East, and certainly never with the mind-set of abandoning their motherland for another.

He:

Ragga socodku waw door
Hadduu moodku daayee
Derbi lama fadhiistiyo
Halkii kuu dartee
Kol haddaan wax daaqiyo
Duunyo iiga foofeyn

Doqoniino weeyaan
Inaga oo isdul joogna.

Waan duulayaaye
Degmooy iisoo ducaya.

Traveling suits a man fine
If death is delayed departing him
He can't shelter
In the warmth of a comforting wall
If there is no gain to be garnered
(And) that livestock is all gone (for good)
It is imbecilic
To wait for a better day!

Would you be able to bless me
(My wife) with a benediction?

She:

Doonyo meel kuu oodnayd
Soo dareerin mayside
Dalkale taad ka dayi layd
Halka nooga dooro

Waynoo danbaysaa Dacaroow,
Ha degdeggine joog.

You will not fling open the gate
To a throng of (livestock)
That of which you are in search of in another
    country
Seek it in your own (still).

Better days are ahead
Please be patient Da'ar.

HIBO NURA AND MOHAMED ADEN DA'AR

A Brief Overview of Somali History

Some sources estimate that Somalis have been in Somalia for two thousand years. Yet the Somalis' own origin stories tell that it was a thousand years ago, perhaps a little less, that Arabs landed on Somali beaches, wandered into the mainland, and married African natives. Thus were born the *Soomaale* (Go Milk for Yourself) souls. There is no definite date on which the country of Somalia was said to be formed. What is understood is that most of what is known about Somali history does not go back much further than the nineteenth century.[1]

During the last quarter of the nineteenth century, Europeans, carelessly disregarding the country's social identity (culture, language, religion, and history), began dismembering the land shared by the *Soomaale* in eastern Africa. From 1827 to 1963, colonial powers divided Somalia into five parts: French Somaliland for France, British Somaliland for Britain, Italian Somaliland for Italy, the Ogaden region of Ethiopia for Ethiopians, and, lastly, in 1963, the Northern Frontier District for Kenya. After ten years of United Nations trusteeship and through Italian efforts "to teach [Somalis] how to be on their own," British Somaliland and Italian Somaliland united under one flag, riding on the winds of freedom sweeping through the continent of Africa in the 1960s. The newly united Somalia established its first-ever government, led by President Aden Abdulla Osman, Prime Minister Abdirashid Ali Sharmarke, a legislative parliamentary body, and a judicial system. This fledgling nation took its first few tentative, wobbly steps on democratic feet.[2]

From the outset, the new nation tried to rally the remaining dismembered parts of Somalia to join in reunification, particularly the Ogaden region of Ethiopia. But the Organization of African Unity—now the African Union—did not support a new wave of boundary quarrels. And

Somali Independence Day

Other than the religious holidays, Somalis gather for one major event: Somali Independence Day. The date celebrates Somalia's independence from colonial British and Italian rule and the founding of the Republic of Somalia in 1960. Though Djibouti commemorates the event on May 27, northern Somalia on June 26, and southern Somalia on July 1, in Minnesota Somalis from Kenya, Djibouti, Ethiopia, and beyond join others from the mainland to celebrate on the weekends between June 20 and July 1. They gather together, dance, and compete in soccer games to honor the memory of their motherland and her independence.

On June 26, 1960, the first Somali flag was hoisted to float and flap in the air. Then on July 1, it was raised in the south of Somalia, and Somalis everywhere sang, danced, and composed ceremonial poems for the occasion. One of the most revered and oldest poets in this nation of poets, Haji Adan Ahmed Hassan (Afqallooc), who lived to the age of 115, contributed to the celebration. He had been imprisoned for his poetic swipes against the British, even held for "sedition" up to the last day of colonial reign. But then Haji-Adan-Afqallooc let loose his words of wisdom to mark the momentous occasion:

> Thank God the flag of asylum has been hoisted
> Like the full moon's light it brightens the earth all around
> It is a verse of mercy that God sent to (us)
> It is a sweet breeze that descends from above.
>
> It is the geyser's origin that quenches the thirst of men
> It is the blooming flower and verdure that is all matured
> (That) of which God delayed but will never devalue . . .

This particular poem, though one of the best, is not among the well known, many of which have been set to music and are performed in annual celebrations of Somali independence.

Dancing to a popular Somali traditional beat, young Somalis celebrate Independence Day.

the Western World, particularly the United States, was not keen on aiding the Somali military against Ethiopia. It was not long before this sore claimed its first causality. In 1964 Prime Minister Sharmarke lost his position following a foreign policy disagreement with President Osman about with whom Somalia should militarily ally itself as it sought to dislodge the Ogaden region from Ethiopia.[3]

The new prime minister, Abdirizak Haji Hussein, focused on institutional building, taking immediate action to curb insidious corruption, attempting to raise ethical standards, and establishing a merit-based employment framework. But this courageous, competent prime minister lasted just two years in office. In 1967, in Somalia's second election, Sharmarke returned to the forefront, claiming the presidency over Osman. And so, the first democratically elected president of Somalia, Aden Abdulla Osman, became the first president on the entire African continent to magnanimously walk away from his office, yielding to the power of the ballot box rather than to bullets. As political scientist Theodore Vestal noted, "Somalia had been the first country in Africa to peacefully replace a government in power through the ballot."[4]

Two years later, on October 15, 1969, the second democratically elected president of Somalia, Sharmarke, was assassinated. Then, on October 21 at 3:00 AM, a group of military elites stormed the prime minister's residence and arrested the cabinet members. The officers who masterminded the coup d'état were led by the uneducated but charismatic oratorical genius General Mohamed Siad Barre. The ordinary public, disappointed in the pace of progress, thronged the streets to celebrate. Siad Barre took advantage of the people's emotions, eloquently saying everything they wanted to hear, but then adopted what he called "Scientific Socialism." He allied himself with the Soviet Union, a monumental disappointment to Somalis

Abdirizak Haji Hussein, former prime minister of Somalia. The authenticity of his leadership for the common good has been attested to by scholars as well as by candid Somalis who have worked closely with him. A rare breed of leader, Abdirizak Haji Hussein passed the test of integrity time and again. One of the savviest self-taught Somalis, at the age of eighty-eight he still follows the whirlwind political turmoil that Somalia is facing, though he now calls Minneapolis home.

of other political leanings. On a more successful tack, in 1972 he introduced the first-ever Somali orthography and announced that the country had chosen the Latin script for the Somali language.[5]

In 1977 Siad Barre, interested along with his fellow citizens in seeing a united Somalia, realized that neighboring Ethiopia was in the midst of immense internal conflict and rushed to capitalize. That summer the Somali army stormed the Ogaden region in support of a rebel group, flexing a Russian-built military muscle that was the envy of Africa. By November "90 percent" of the land Somalis had been laying claim to for a little more than a century was in their control. Ethiopia conceded.[6]

The victory did not last long, however, as Somalia's former ally, the Soviet Union, abruptly switched its allegiance to support Ethiopia. As the Soviet military began fighting side by side with the Ethiopians, Siad Barre sought assistance from the Americans and the British. Initially, both countries offered much-needed financial support that would help Somalia detach from its dependence on the Soviet bloc. With miscalculated haste, Barre prematurely cut diplomatic ties with the Soviet Union, but in retaliation the Soviets unleashed a major military airlift of advisors, parachuting them right into the middle of the Ogaden region. Outnumbered and outgunned, the Somali army suffered enormous losses. Outside help never arrived. Once the war was lost, however, the United States began flooding Somalia with light arms insufficient to challenge the Soviet-supplied Ethiopians. In the end, Barre had to withdraw his army in humiliation.[7]

The fallout from defeat adversely affected the regime's stance throughout the following decade. Soon Barre, once the country's most feared man, was openly criticized, the largest population of refugees in the world flooded to Somalia from Ethiopia, and the vanquished army mutinied. Trying to contain the discontent, Barre had several high-ranking officers executed. Talk of revolution continued, and then in April 1978 a group of military officers, mostly from the central and northeastern clan of Majeerteen, attempted the first coup. Most of the leaders were caught and hastily executed. The survivors fled to Ethiopia to organize an armed opposition, the Somalia Salvation Democratic Front. Siad Barre turned his wrath on Majeerteen civilians, scorching cities, villages, and nomadic compounds, mining wells, and slaughtering livestock.[8]

Meanwhile, as northerners realized the magnitude of economic and human rights abuses the regime had inflicted

Somali Clan Tree

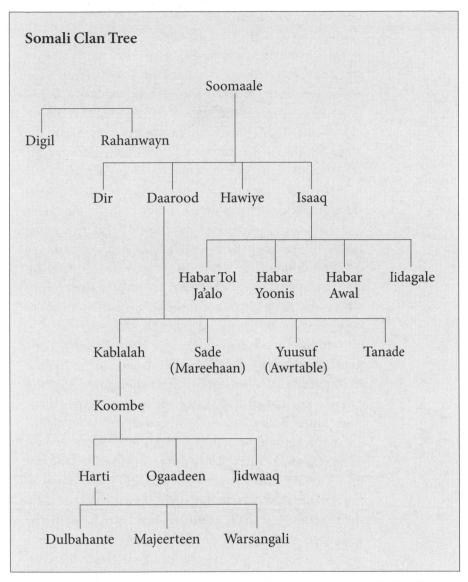

This clan tree highlights Soomaale, the mythical patriarchal figure who, it has been said, fathered four of the six largest Somali clans. His descendants, through Dir, Daarood, Hawiye, and Isaaq, are today called *Somalis*. Members of two other major Somali clans, Digil and Rahanwayn, are traditionally agriculturalists. Note: Somali groups not shown here include minorities such as Benadaris, Barawans, Bantus, and Gaboye. Said S. Samatar, *Oral Poetry and Somali Nationalism: The Case of Sayyid Maḥ ammad Abdille Ḥasan* (Cambridge: Cambridge University Press, 1982), 10.

upon them, a volcano of unrest exploded into the streets of major cities. A second armed opposition, the Somali National Movement, composed exclusively of the northwest Isaaq clan, debilitated and depleted the national army in the north, sowing the seeds for Siad Barre's final defeat. Other groups followed suit: the Hawiye clan from the central region created the United Somali Congress in 1988, and the Digil/Mirifle of the Rahanwayn clan from the south/southwest organized the Somali Democratic Movement.[9]

Somalia had divided itself, and Siad Barre was able to use tribalism as his deadliest weapon. Beginning in the center and then moving to the northeast and north before working his way to the south, Barre targeted the clans one by one as other tribes stood by. Still, despite years of brutal attacks on the civilian population, Siad Barre's hold on power eventually dissipated. In January 1991, alone and with no army left to protect him, he was forced to flee Mogadishu.[10]

Into the vacuum two prominent United Somali Congress members, Mohamed Farrah Aidid and Ali Mahdi, emerged as a pair of butchers, brutally fighting over the poisoned bait of a ravaged city. Vicious, arbitrary attacks were aimed at the Daarood clan, considered to be the regime's prime support, and the fighting spilled over into the entire south. The violent clashes contaminated the rest of the nation, and soon the drought, misery, and mercilessness were exposed to the world as mothers cried over their children's skeletal, malnourished bodies. Southerners began to pour into the neighboring countries, and northerners, disgusted and despairing, declared secession. Nonprofit organizations rushed to aid the hungry, but they were hamstrung by the warlords and their minions. The United Nations sent peacekeepers to feed the children, but Aidid and Mahdi intimidated the U.N. representatives. Though donated aid poured in, the militia looted the delivery trucks at will while babies and children died.[11]

When it seemed that all hope was lost, suddenly the

world's most powerful nation declared it would send 27,000 troops to Mogadishu. During his last days in office, in December 1992, U.S. President George H. W. Bush decided to feed the Somali children. Others from around the world, twenty-four countries in all, eagerly joined in the effort. Armed with a U.N. Security Council mandate to use military means if necessary to ensure that humanitarian aid reached the needy and to bring about a political resolution, the troops beached in Mogadishu. Operation Restore Hope swelled into a multinational military force 37,000 strong that descended on southern Somalia, establishing a secured zone and feeding the starving children.[12]

Still, the political fiasco continued to sizzle as Aidid and Mahdi refused to let up, wasting whatever goodwill the rest of the world was ready to bestow on Somalia. Peace was impossible in Mogadishu, and, along with it, the entire southern part of Somalia seethed. Then, when Mahdi finally opted to negotiate with the world, Aidid's camp ambushed fifteen Pakistani peacekeepers. U.S. Navy SEALs were sent to apprehend Aidid, whose fighters successfully shot down two Black Hawk helicopters. Eighteen American service members, along with hundreds of Somalis, lost their lives, and one serviceman's body, dragged through the streets of Mogadishu, was viewed by millions on the TV news. The mission to capture Aidid turned into a disaster both for Somalis and for America's psyche. Soon thereafter, on March 25, 1994, President Bill Clinton ordered all Americans out of Somalia. Again, the rest of the world followed.[13]

Somalia was left to wallow in its self-inflicted wounds. Aidid managed to spoil the golden political and economic opportunities to rebuild the nation at the same time that he spoiled Somalia for the history books by turning the international community's goodwill into an infamy made famous by the movie and the book *Black Hawk Down*. Beyond this incident, the world hardly remembers the thousands of unnamed, unknown dead Somalis.[14]

In total, twenty-one years of a repressive regime's ruthless war on its people, followed by the brutalities orchestrated by the warlords, made the country, particularly the south, a hellhole of violence. The toll on the lives of the general populace was unbearable. With danger all around, the citizens had no alternative but to get out of harm's way, and they fled the cities. The majority trusted their feet to carry them to safety, trekking to Ethiopia and Kenya in lines that stretched to the horizon. At times, as rain poured down, nights became indistinguishable from days. Soon, those who had once cheated death were overtaken by hunger and exhaustion. Others lost their lives trying to sail to Yemen on precariously unsafe boats. An estimated one to two million Somalis escaped to neighboring countries.[15]

On Foot in Fear

> *Naftu orod bay kugu aamintaa*
> Life (in danger) trusts only running!
>
> SOMALI PROVERB

As Somalis fled the south, they knew not where they were heading nor how long they were going to be away from their homes. Misery was their constant companion. One example is the story of Dr. Amina Siyad, who paid the last penny of her family savings to procure a small fishing dhow in May 1991. Along with ninety others, she and her two young daughters fled to Mombasa, Kenya. Miles into the Indian Ocean, the boat ran out of fuel. Ten days later, now sick and starving, the refugees finally reached shore by wind sailing. Alas, Kenyan authorities refused to allow them to disembark, keeping them in limbo for another nine days before forcing them to sail back to Mogadishu.

There, Dr. Siyad could hardly withstand the horrors of death, destruction, and danger all around her. In November she managed to get a flight to the northeastern city of Bosaso, where she and her daughters reunited with her husband, who had escaped earlier. "Eventually," she stated, "from Bosaso, along with many other displaced people from the southern region, we crossed by [a] boat to the refugee camp in Yemen." She concluded, "Having first sought survival, we now sought life," a new life in Yemen.[16]

At this time, Somali writer and Nobel Prize for Literature nominee Nuruddin Farah was teaching in Kampala, Uganda. Farah, who rushed to meet the fleeing refugees, among them many members of his family, enumerated the sheer magnitude of the devastation on the faces of those he had met in the camps in his nonfiction book, *Yesterday, Tomorrow: Voices from the Somali Diaspora*. He begins with a gripping narrative: "I remembered the renegade tears coursing down the refugees' cheeks. My younger sister had been in the first boatload of Somalis to arrive in Bombasa . . . Other than my immediate family, I ran into other Somalis in Mombasa's refugee camp, escapees who had brought along with them damaged memories. Time and time again they spoke of the terror which they had lived through, their demeanor undignified, their eyes mournful, their temperament as runny as the lachrymal catarrh affecting the uncared-for orphan."[17]

The choice to travel from north to south or from south to north depended on what time one left or to what clan one belonged. But, as the Somali adage asserts, in such danger, it is best to trust only one's own feet: "just run" was the motto playing in the refugees' minds. Finally reaching camps on the Kenyan border, they found their place of refuge to be burdened with horror, psychological trauma, physical and sexual attacks on women, poor sanitation, and lack of food. As Abdikadir Jama, a father of five whose home is now in Minneapolis, tells,

I was born and raised in Erigavo, a city at the tip of the northern part of Somalia. I left for Mogadishu

Distinctive Somali Traits

Though the following may sound like a dose of vanity, Somalis' socially distinctive traits of bravery, beauty, poetic prowess, and pride have been noted. It is said that Somalis have no fear of fighting: British journalist Richard Dowden stated, "One abiding, horrifying but typical image [of Somalis' bravery] stays in mind: a young Somali dressed in T-shirt, flop-flops and *macawiis,* the traditional skirt-like wrap, running at a American armoured Humvee, firing an AK47 from the hip. Bravery, ten points. Stupidity, also ten points. He was cut to shreds." Another British writer, Gerald Hanley, embraced the war-prone nature of Somalis as a reckless pride, a warrior-like mentality. In his book *Warriors: Life and Death Among the Somalis,* he stated, "of all the races of Africa there cannot be one better to live among than the most difficult, the proudest, the bravest, the vainest, the most merciless, the friendliest; the Somalis."[i]

Somalis' garrulous, argumentative conversational style has also been highlighted by those who encountered them. Dowden, again, noted, "I once tried to argue with a Somali friend . . . As the discussion developed she simply reiterated her argument more stridently. She changed down a gear and tried to drive straight over my argument, crushing [it] under a pounding of words that grew louder and louder. Later, after I spent a longer time in Somalia, I realized that she was not being rude, she was being Somali. Challenge, fight, win."[ii]

Beauty, though always in the eye of the beholder, is an asset of which Somali women own their share. Through their racist lenses, even the Fascist Italians in the 1930s admired Somali women's desirability while denying their African identity. "[I]t was almost universally agreed [in Italy] that Somali [women] were the most desirable in a sense because their beauty was believed to be only an exaggeration of whiteness," argues Beverly Allen, a professor of French, Italian, and Comparative Literature at Syracuse University.[iii]

More recently, in the late seventies, Iman, a Somali native, dazzled the world with her captivating looks. For almost twenty years she reigned supreme on the Western runways, touting the title of supermodel, the first black woman to do so, paving the way for other women of color. Known for her singular first name, Iman wooed the world not only through her supreme beauty but also through her confidence and her adherence to her Somali identity. She was followed by the gorgeous Waris Dirie, another supermodel who graced the world's most prized magazine covers. As Islam discourages women from flaunting their beauty, it's not surprising that both were discovered by accident, neither at the same time nor by the same person.[iv]

And, poetry. Somalis' capacity to masterfully weave words into pure, poetic composition in no less than seven forms lives on, although no stanzas older than two centuries have survived. Somalis are able to metrically message and curve words into smoothly aligned verses, flowing from an elevated, logical argument obedient to an alliterative system from start to end. Their expressive nature synthesizes and condenses thoughts into poetry. Somalis have long been known to capture accounts of their affairs in waves of measured words, grieving about the tumult of time's uncertainties as well celebrating its serenity. Historically, poetry has been the medium for cogent communication that would carry news, nominate leaders, announce and at times cause wars that lasted decades. For that, Somalis worship, fear, and admire poetry all at once.[v]

Finally, with characteristic pride and an assertive attitude Somalis mastered the tenacity to confront adversities and to lower the threshold for tolerating ill treatment. Somali individuals are inclined to react publicly if they feel their faith has been slighted or dishonored. Thus, in Minne-

Said Salah Ahmed, known to Somalis as Said Salah, is one of the foremost Somali playwrights and poets, a producer who has distinguished himself with his careful, uncanny sensibility into the social psyche. He is a proud messenger who has sworn to carry the baton of teaching the Somali language. Said entered the performing arts arena to spread his passion for the power of words, particularly Somali poetry, because "as a teacher, a classroom was not enough for me." His finely honed craft, based in history with traces of nomadic life, focuses on social justice. He teaches the Somali language at the University of Minnesota.

sota and other states, Somalis have walked away from jobs, united en masse, and other times mounted legal challenges, mostly involving disagreements about prayer time or place, but about respect for their rights, too.[vi]

Despite the dire conditions in their motherland and around the globe, Somali pride has not dimmed. A Somali still argues with anyone and everyone, still spends his last penny in excess, and still is confrontational. But there is balance: Somalis are also known for their selfless hospitality and unguarded generosity.

but evacuated in January 1991 to the southern tip of Somalia, Kismayo. Once again, in March 1992, we had to flee Kismayo from where we then sojourned a year. I was so disturbed and befuddled with our circumstance that I did not know where we were running to. But I recall now that we ended up crossing the border to Kenya, to a small camp there. After a while, I left the camp, and through Nairobi got to yet another camp in Mombasa. In that place, though it was safer than others that we have heard about, death was a daily companion. Children, in particular, were falling down dead like flies from countless diseases. When they were not dying, they were suffering from lack of care or food. It simply seemed that they were even dying from drinking water.

The Somalis of Minnesota are mostly remnants of that ruin, driven from their country by indescribable violence.[18]

War (News) Center in San Diego

"Immigrants are a very mobile population . . . They freely move [to] wherever the economy allows them to get a job or social service agencies exist to help them adjust to life in the U.S. or where a large group of others from their country live."

BARBARA J. RONNINGEN, MINNESOTA STATE DEMOGRAPHICS CENTER

In 1988, with Siad Barre aerially bombarding northern Somalia and killing off his own people, the first exodus of northern Somalis began. They sought refuge in neighboring countries, most in Ethiopia, others in Djibouti and Yemen. Some of the survivors eventually made their way west, settling in Europe and Canada. One destination not

in the running was the United States, which fully sup-
ported Barre's repressive regime with both financial and
military means right up to the end of the Cold War in
1989. Only after the collapse of the communist bloc did
the United States finally take action against Barre's massive human rights violations by cutting off all aid to his
regime. Even as the airwaves brought heartbreaking news
of the erupting humanitarian crisis, it took almost three
more years for Somali refugees to be recognized as such,
thus designating them for resettlement. Earlier, in the
mid-1980s, Somali-Ethiopians who had fled to Somalia
right after the Somali-Ethiopian war of 1977 were the only
ethnic Somalis with recognized refugee status. The majority of these Somalis who came to America made their way
to San Diego, California.

When the United States recognized the unfolding humanitarian crises in Somalia, voluntary agencies, or
VOLAGs, such as the International Rescue Committee,
Lutheran Social Services, and Catholic Charities, began as-
sessing Somalis in refugee camps for resettlement to several
countries but mainly to the United States. The VOLAGs,
with years of experience in resettlement following the
Vietnam War, usually preferred to place new arrivals in
areas where their compatriots were already concentrated.
But in the early days of resettlement, only San Diego had
a community of Somali refugees, and not all the newcomers could be placed there. Deeply distraught about the
loss of their nation, burdened by the still-raging civil war
back home, the first Somali refugees arrived in Arizona,
Connecticut, Georgia, Illinois, Maryland, Massachusetts,
Michigan, Missouri, Nebraska, New York, North Carolina,
Ohio, Pennsylvania, Texas, Virginia, and Wisconsin at the
beginning of 1990s. They did not begin to resettle in Minnesota until 1993.

The Office of Homeland Security shows that twenty-
five Somalis arrived in America for resettlement in 1990;

the next year, their numbers increased to 192. In 1993, however, the total jumped to 1,570. The largest number arrived in San Diego because "a handful of Somali families from the Ogaden region of Ethiopia were already there," the weather was similar to that of their homeland, and agencies in that city had the experience to deliver services. Those who were not able to reach San Diego took the next best option: establishing a line of communication with the Somali community there. The city became the capital of the Somali news center, where *war* about livability, job opportunities, political asylum, resettlement, and the best service providers was traded.[19]

Both the established Somali American community and the new arrivals in San Diego faced a scarcity of jobs in the early 1990s. One discouraged Somali case manager, Abdi Husen, who was working for a resettlement agency and later became a successful businessman in Minneapolis, remembered, "as I picked many of [the newly arrived refugees] up from the airport, I would drop them off to residential apartments in southeast San Diego, but would cringe in pain. In pain, because the reality of the life they would encounter firsthand in America was far from the one they had imagined." Abdi painted a bleak picture of the economically disadvantaged neighborhoods, adding, "[it] is not an exaggeration that . . . I became frightened for them, too. Frightened because, if I, though one of the luckiest few with

---

New Arrivals in America

Hiss Ahmed Ismail:

I came to San Diego in 1992, went to high school there, and once I was done with it I began taking classes at a community college but was very discouraged by the lack of employment opportunities. What made it harder was that I was getting calls from relatives in refugee camps and in Somalia [asking for help]. I had a part-time library job, three hours a day, but it would take me another three hours to get there and back, spending a whole six hours a day altogether. I was tired of it.

Hodon Adan:

I arrived in San Diego in 1992. I was thinking that I was going to save the rest of my family, at least those who made it out and were in refugee camps. I thought jobs and money were not going to be the things to worry about anymore. But that was not what greeted me in San Diego. The most discouraging signs were that the people who were there when we came were already disillusioned. There were no jobs. That really worried me sick.[vii]

a college degree and a good command of the English language, was fighting with my own demons of doubt, how would a single mother ... of six or more with neither the educational background nor employable skills, survive?" His account was validated by many others.[20]

A Ray of Hope

In early summer 1992, a poultry company called Heartland Food Company in Marshall, Minnesota, added a third shift to its turkey processing plant and sought staff to fill it. On May 20, 1992, the Sioux Falls, South Dakota, *Argus Leader* included an advertisement that the plant was hiring. Four Somalis from Sioux Falls showed up at Heartland the very next day. They were hired on the spot and told that overtime was available: if they had friends, they should come apply, too.

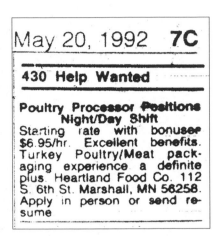

May 20, 1992   7C

430 Help Wanted

Poultry Processor Positions Night/Day Shift Starting rate with bonuses $6.95/hr. Excellent benefits. Turkey Poultry/Meat packaging experience a definite plus. Heartland Food Co. 112 S. 6th St. Marshall, MN 56258. Apply in person or send resume

Where it all began: Heartland Food Company's "help wanted" ad in the *Argus Leader,* May 20, 1992.

The word these four sent back to Sioux Falls was pleasantly surprising: all four, even with their poor English and lack of experience, had been hired immediately. Furthermore, the plant needed more people, and it was processing poultry, not pork. This headline trickled to the center of the Somali *war*-mill in San Diego. Questions about the *war*'s reliability remained, yet the news persisted. After two months, it was time to send out a team of scouts to test the validity of this glimmer of hope rising from Marshall, Minnesota.[21]

The Ultimate *Sahan* Group

Hot on the faint trail of *war* about jobs, four bachelors from San Diego hopped into a car. Just as their nomad forefathers

Halal and Haraam

Halal means permissible and *haraam* means the opposite, forbidden. These two words are used to differentiate between various ways of life and produce such as meat, drink, and pharmaceutical products. Haraam are pork and all items or products that derive from pork; animals that are not slaughtered properly in accordance with religious teachings; birds of prey; carnivorous animals; alcohol; and any foods containing these products.

Durdur Bakery and Grocery: a halal mini-market and one of the thriving Somali-owned businesses in South Minneapolis.

Halal items on sale in Durdur.

had traveled in search of greener pastures for thousands of years, this *sahan* group from San Diego was charged with authenticating the news. Abdicadir Abucar Ga'al, a polyglot who speaks four languages, was asked to be the community's eyes and ears. He became the group's leader because the others knew neither the landscape nor the language nor much about driving. After thirty-two hours, most of those with Abdicadir behind the wheel, they reached Sioux Falls but were met with the news that their journey was not yet over. Fortified with a lunch of delicious Somali food, soon they found their way to Marshall's poultry processing plant. Although close to thirty other Somalis were already employed there, all four were hired on the spot.[22]

As *sahan* in Somali culture dictates, the first group of scouts would have aggregated the risks against the ultimate economic advantages and then endorsed community relocation once a greener pasture was confirmed. But this case brought a twist to that central, cultural piece: back home they would have traveled on foot or on horseback to share their good news, but now, in this new country, they delivered it by telephone. Jobs were available in Marshall, Minnesota. And when yet another group from San Diego, this time numbering three, followed and its members were hired, too, the confirmation bell rang even louder. Soon, the exciting and hopeful *war* was being spoken in every ear. Calls reverberated throughout the community, bringing long-awaited hope. They were urged on by the wails of loved ones in refugee camps and the gnawing cries back in Somalia. Some asked for money to feed themselves and their families, others to be plucked from the hell their homes had turned into, still others groused about the harsh life they were forced to endure. Now, anybody who was seeking work or ways to support one's family was heading to Marshall or thinking about how to get there.

In the early 1990s, when Somalis were arriving in the

United States from refugee camps around the world, the country was facing an economic slide, a recession that caused a popular Gulf War president, George H. W. Bush, to lose his reelection bid to Bill Clinton, a relatively unknown governor of a small southern state. In a weak economy, often immigrants, both legal and illegal, are the first to be blamed for draining the employment reservoir. The ill-prepared Somalis, who had heard only about how wealthy Americans are, had met the apathy of joblessness in California and other states. The daily dose of bad news from their homeland and from family members stranded around the globe compounded their desperation but also intensified their resolve to search for greener pastures.[23]

At the height of the recession in 1992, the national unemployment rate was 7.5 percent. In Minnesota it was much lower: 5.6 percent. And though it rose a bit in Minnesota in 1993 to 6.0 percent, it kept sliding back down again and at one point, in 1998, reached as low as 2.8 percent. According to the state demographic center, in the 1990s Minnesota was creating jobs two times faster than its population was growing. On top of that, in the southwestern and western

---

Finding Their Way to Marshall

Safiya Ahmed Dirir:

I was [in San Diego] for four agonizing months when the news that there were jobs in a city called Marshall reached me . . . Prior to it I did not work a day. So I was in despair that most of it was emanating from the fact that I left a large family behind: my sister, her husband and children, my brothers and both of my parents. I promised them that I was going to save them. Well, my friend and I got on a bus sometime in October 1993 from San Diego, arrived in Marshall on a Saturday, were hired the same day, and started working at the turkey poultry plant that following Monday.

Abdihakim Ugas Aden Hadis:

I came to Minnesota where I had heard about good things. I was not disappointed. There were jobs everywhere. The temporary agency that hired us also connected us to transportation that would take a percent off your earnings but would get you to and from work. And though I did not start at the turkey poultry plant at Marshall, I ended up going there.[viii]

---

counties the population was aging, making a shortage in the workforce imminently apparent.

Probably due to their nomadic survival instincts, Somalis found the right state at the right time in which to survive. And fortunately for them, the Minnesota economy kept growing faster than the economy in the rest of the country, while the number of Somalis coming from other states as well as from refugee camps continued to rise faster there than elsewhere.

Once Somalis came to Minnesota, multiple factors—a better job market, a lower cost of living, and a higher minimum wage than in most other states—added to the state's allure. "Making decent wages in California, yes, I was a rare exception to the Somali rule. But once I arrived in Minnesota, I calculated my earnings against my expenses and, with overtime, realized that I could come out ahead, saving," said Abdicadir Ga'al. Hassan Ali Mohamed concurred: "Soon after I arrived in Minneapolis from Kansas, I got a job with a car rental company. And though this was the state minimum wage, it was a lot higher than what I was making there."[24]

After cashing checks and sometimes saving a bit, Somalis in Minnesota were able to soothe their emotional pain by sending a large portion of their earnings to loved ones and by searching for ways to bring them here. Some contacted Minnesota voluntary agencies, asking for assistance for their family members by whatever means available—reunification, sponsorship, or resettlement. Soon these many possibilities were spreading along the Somali *war*-mill.[25]

Table 1:
Unemployment Rates in Minnesota

YEAR	UNEMPLOYMENT RATE
1990	5.8 percent
1991	6.4 percent
1992	5.7 percent
1993	6.0 percent
1994	4.5 percent
1995	5.4 percent
1996	5.4 percent
1997	4.3 percent
1998	2.8 percent
1999	3.1 percent
2000	3.0 percent

Source: Minnesota Department of Economic Security, Research and Statistics office, 2000

Celebrating nomadic roots: two Somali boys enjoy a camel ride at Pillsbury Avenue and West Lake Street in Minneapolis.

The Marshall, Minnesota, group is credited with encouraging members of the new Somali community to withstand the cold weather and hold on to their jobs while working with the VOLAGs to help with sponsorship of family members still lingering in the refugee camps.

Abdi Husen elaborated, "You can't underestimate the price of relative information . . . Some of [it] was already in [the San Diego group's] hands or just close by at the reservoir *war* with the older Somali community of Ethiopian origin in San Diego, who themselves had learned it from the more educated and experienced, the Ethiopians. Once a family or two were brought in, the chain of *war*, again, spread like a wildfire."[26]

Husen had worked for an experienced resettlement and emergency relief agency in East Africa, the International

Rescue Committee (IRC), which had started assisting Ethiopians and Somalis as far back as the 1980s. The Minneapolis businessman had been born in the Somali region of Ethiopia but was raised and educated in Somalia. He asserts that the San Diego group not only was the major artery from which Somalis flowed into Minnesota, thanks to its *war* bugle about jobs, but also was responsible for alerting the local voluntary agencies to the needs of new arrivals. Now Catholic Charities, Lutheran Social Services, the Minnesota Council of Churches, the International Institute of Minnesota, and other resettlement agencies began to see the disastrous proportions of the Somali crisis.

Exceptions to the Rule

While most Somalis found their way to Minnesota through job opportunities in the southern portion of the state, a group of scholars came on their own and before most Minnesotans had even heard of Somalia. Others arrived during the first waves of resettlement. Unlike the rest of the diaspora, this elite group imported a rare commodity: their expertise.

The first to arrive was Nuruddin Farah, a world-renowned Somali writer, perennial nominee for the Nobel Prize in Literature, and recipient of the Neustadt International Prize for Literature. Farah came to Minneapolis in 1987 and taught at the University of Minnesota the following spring. He was later named to the university's Winton Chair in the Liberal Arts. Though he lives in South Africa, he frequently visits the North Star State and jokes about Minnesota being his second home.

Similarly, the "Samatar Brothers," as they are known in Somali circles, were attracted to Minnesota's institutions of higher learning. Abdi I. Samatar, who arrived in 1992, teaches geography at the University of Minnesota. He is known for his admirable body of scholarly work and two classic books, *The State and Rural Transformation in Northern Somalia, 1884–1986* and *An African Miracle: State and Class Leadership and Colonial Legacy in Botswana Development.* Ahmed I. Samatar, who arrived in St. Paul in 1994 to serve as the dean of an ambitious international studies program at Macalester College, founded the Institute for Global Citizenship there. He has lectured throughout the world at many prestigious scholarly institutions, and, as a prodigious writer and the author of the significant work *Socialist Somalia: Rhetoric and Reality,* he is considered the Somalis' leading scholar.

Finally, Cawo Mohamed Abdi, assistant professor of sociology at the University of Minnesota, is likewise an accomplished academic author. Professor Abdi came to Minnesota to write her PhD dissertation on human migration, and now it seems she is here to stay.[ix]

An unknown number of Somalis, arriving in Minnesota on their own, had become self-sufficient without intervention from social service agencies, and records indicate that the number of Somalis relocating directly from refugee camps began slowly, with 121 people in 1993. According to the Minnesota Department of Human Services, the number of refugees was very close to 5,000, but an unofficial estimate of the number of Somalis in Minnesota

---

Why Minnesota?

Minnesota's hospitality to refugees goes back as far as 1948, when the Displaced Persons Act was signed into law and the state opened its borders to Latvians and Estonians displaced by World War II. Again in 1975, following the Vietnam War, Minnesota began accepting Vietnamese and other Southeast Asians, who, fearing death or persecution, left their homelands by foot and boat, creating "a massive humanitarian disaster" that would continue into the 1980s.[x]

Further, as Minneapolis mayor, Hubert Humphrey had muscled together the strongest and first Fair Employment Practices Commission in the country and established the city's Committee on Human Relations to protect minorities, particularly African Americans and Jews, in 1947. Humphrey went on to serve as U.S. senator and vice president, and along the way his progressive program of equal employment opportunity, fair housing, lunch counter service, and public transportation were monumental gifts to Minnesota and to the country. This legacy expanded when Minnesotan Walter Mondale joined Humphrey's staff, becoming his ally in the struggle to overturn injustice and inequality in America.[xi]

When the two politicians led calls for a change in policy regarding Southeast Asia, Congress passed the Refugee Assistance Act in 1975. It appropriated funds in part to assist local human services agencies in resettling the displaced in the United States as well as to provide aid to the United Nations High Commissioner for Refugees based on humanitarian grounds. Minnesota and California were the two primary states to which Southeast Asian refugees were directed.

The act was set to expire in the summer of 1977, but Humphrey and Mondale, by then himself U.S. vice president, intervened, and the legislation was extended for three more years. Most importantly, that step paved the way for the two most essential elements of today's refugee resettlement policy. First, it solidified federal support for domestic social services rendered by local volunteer agencies. Second, it acknowledged the need to attend to humanitarian crises that arose outside of the United States. In 1980, a revised version of the act based eligibility for refugee resettlement in the United States on imminent personal danger within one's own country.[xii]

This inclusive political environment has fostered a tolerant climate, nurturing *martisoor* seeds to establish roots in Minnesota. Somalis and many refugee groups before them feel welcomed. Job opportunities for new arrivals enhance their financial outlook, and stable housing helps them feel settled, raising the possibility of healing and eventually building back what the refugees have lost—their pride.

Confederation of Somali Community in Minnesota

The oldest and most prominent Somali social service center, Confederation of Somali Community in Minnesota (CSCM) is housed in Minneapolis's Brian Coyle Center, just steps to the west of the high-rise apartments at Riverside Plaza known to some as "Little Mogadishu." The center is easily accessible to residents of Riverside Plaza, who make up the largest concentration of Somalis in the state. CSCM is run by the unassuming Saeed Fahia, a scientist with a master's degree in physics and a doctorate in education. Although he taught physics and served as associate dean of academic affairs at the National University of Somalia at Lafoole, Fahia has never used his doctoral title, nor is he known for it.

Today Fahia gracefully holds his position as executive director of CSCM. With his mild manner and soft-spoken insights, Fahia is able to neutralize simmering tensions by simply applying his most effective virtue—patience. For example, when United Nations special representative to Somalia Ahmedou Ould-Abdallah paid a visit to Minnesota in July 2008, the CSCM center was percolating with tension stirred by clan-minded groups jockeying for position to meet him. Some were trying to gain favor from Fahia, others accused him of siding with one group, and still others did not want him to be the peacemaker, period. In the end, Fahia managed to satisfy all sides.

As a result of his calm leadership, CSCM has served the community in the largest way and for the longest time. It offers a variety of services ranging from advice on immigration matters, divorce mediation, social advocacy, and political education to youth activities, art, and entertainment. And though the center has been plagued by budget cuts, it still delivers these services across multiple generations, in English or in Somali or in a combination of the two. While Fahia is usually found shepherding haphazardly shaped lines of people to his office in the morning hours, he remains at work late into the evening as well. Financial strains have resulted in fewer staff and longer lines, yet CSCM lives up to its mission statement: "To strengthen the capacity of Somalis in Minnesota to become contributing members of society, while preserving their culture."

Dr. Saeed Fahia, executive director of Confederation of Somali Community in Minnesota, at his office in a rare moment of respite.

was grossly larger—60,000 to 70,000 in 2000—due to the secondary migration. Soon after 1993, Somalis began establishing social service agencies, among them the Confederation of Somali Community in Minnesota, African Community Services, Somali Action Alliance, Somali Benadiri Community of Minnesota, and Somali Mai Community of Minnesota, so that they could offer resettlement assistance to their own.[27]

The Somalis who settled in Marshall began the push for more resources and improved working conditions. They soon collided with management at the poultry plant. In September 1993, eighty-two walked off the job in response to the rumor that a Somali man had been unfairly fired. As a result, all of the protesters were themselves fired. They took their skills to other meat and poultry plants, in Manchester, Pelican Rapids, and Willmar, Minnesota, and in Storm Lake, Iowa. Still, Marshall remained the magnet, where newcomers would start first.[28]

As the number of Somalis arriving from San Diego surged, the *war* about jobs spread wider and into other states. Minnesota continued to absorb this eager, migrating labor force which, in the process, discovered a host of other employment opportunities. Those who found work in the hospitality industry, rental car businesses, and janitorial services or as food and beverage servers, parking lot attendants, taxi drivers, and assembly-line workers were soon followed by social services providers, teachers, accountants, interpreters, businesspeople and entrepreneurs, and workers in the semiconductor industry, hired at such companies as Seagate, Honeywell, ADC, and IBM. The more their numbers grew, the larger the pool of employment opportunities and the better their choices became.

It did not take long for skilled professionals to learn of the rapidly rising Somali population in Minnesota and to decide to reestablish themselves in the Midwest.

Dr. Abdirahman Mohamed, the first medically licensed Somali family physician in Minnesota, has worn multiple hats within his clinic, serving as psychiatrist, psychologist, sociologist, community leader, religious expert, rights advocate, and educator and guide to both Somalis and Americans serving Somalis. Dr. Mohamed, presently at the helm of Axis Medical Center, a nonprofit clinic whose clientele is mostly Somalis in South Minneapolis, described the path that brought him to Minnesota:

> Once I was done with my fellowship in global health at John Hopkins, as well as earning a master's of public health at University of Maryland, I was offered an associate professorship at a number of [reputable] higher education institutions such as John Hopkins, the University of Maryland, and my alma mater, the University of Illinois College of Medicine, but I chose Minnesota when my uncle called me and said, "I am calling your bluff.

Prominent Somali medical doctor Mohamed Abdirahman Hassan. Dr. Mohamed, as Somalis call him, is a professor at the University of Minnesota's medical school specializing in gastroenterology, hepatology, and nutrition. Dr. Mohamed speaks Italian, English, and Somali. He studied each of the languages in the capitals of their respective countries.

You always said you wanted to go back to Somalia [and serve your people], but Somalia came to you. Somalia is in Minnesota." So despite all these tempting opportunities, [in 1999] I came here, where I am always the proudest when I pass on a piece of valuable health-related information to a person who needs it the most.[29]

Dr. Mohamed understands his particular role in the community. "What is so invaluable about a Somali physician's service to a Somali patient is that the essential doctor/patient trust is not only the verbal communication but the cultural language, too. The core of the relationship is that of how a Somali speaks to his/her physician, that he/she tells his/her concern first. The physician just listens until the patient exhausts his/her list. Somalis are not trained in the simple direct answer/questions format. And a Somali physician knows that."[30]

Dr. Fozia Abrar, the first medically licensed female Somali medical doctor in Minnesota, told a similar story, adding her perspective on the community.

> I came here in 1999 looking for a fellowship in occupational environmental medicine at the University of Minnesota. Primarily, however, I wanted to be in Minnesota because of the large Somali community. I was yearning to serve the single mothers who had left a ruined nation and possibly most of their families behind. My hope for Somalis in Minnesota is high. I believe they are rapidly approaching the bridge to assimilation. I am proud of the first-generation Somali Americans who mostly were about ten years old or younger when they got here but now are scaling up the ladder with education, particularly girls. You can see and watch how far they have acculturated, yet [they are] self-assertively holding on to their motherland traits with gratitude.[31]

Others, like Abdulla Mohamed, a pharmacology graduate student who moved from Houston, followed the flock for another reason: "I had no problem managing life [in Texas], but my wife has a family here and wanted to be close. I had to accommodate for her desire."[32]

With the Minnesota resettlement agencies involved,

others, like the Somali Benadiris from Mogadishu, were brought directly to Minnesota from refugee camps. In May 1996, Mohamed Abuker Haji Hussein, formerly an English professor at the National University of Lafoole, now director of Somali Benadiri Community, along with his wife and two children flew in to Minneapolis ahead of the rest of the Somali Benadiri group. Hussein, with his educational background and facility in English, was brought in first so that he could assist others in their resettlement. Twenty-one days later, twenty families followed. The flow of Somali Benadiris coming to Minnesota from refugee camps soon surpassed the four thousand mark, Hussein asserts. And, just like other groups of Somalis, Benadiris attracted others to the state as a secondary migration. Hussein estimates that close to one-fourth of all Somalis in Minnesota are Somali Benadiris. Members of this group are known for their independent business-minded skills. Once in Minneapolis, it did not take long for them to put down roots and employ their expertise. They have established a number of restaurants, including the only Somali "chain"—Qoraxlow in Minneapolis—*halwo* (sweets) businesses, and henna artist studios.[33]

As the Somali community grew, Minnesota quickly became a home away from home. Engineer Abdi Mohamoud Suleiman clarifies:

Somali Benadiri Community of Minnesota

Benadiri—or "people of Mogadishu," mostly Arab descendants with a legitimate claim to the capital city—have as a group been among the most unfortunate victims of the Somali civil war. Though they belong to no particular clan, they were brutally mistreated, robbed of property and birthright, and raped of body and soul. Consequently, a large number of Benadiri sought refuge outside of Somalia, and some found their way to Minnesota. Under the leadership of Mohamed Abuker Haji Hussein, director of the Somali Benadiri Community of Minnesota, they are thriving. Despite the difficulties they have endured, their resilience makes other Somalis proud.

My family and I were doing fine in New Jersey, where we bought a house after I had returned from the Middle East. Then my oldest daughter came to Minnesota to go to Carleton College. I came to see her in 2009, and on my way back to New Jersey I stayed with a cousin who asked me to work on a project with him for five months. Then I thought, here was a chance for my younger ones, too, to mingle with other Somalis [in Minnesota], perhaps learn some Somali language and catch up with a bit of their ancestral heritage.[34]

Mohamed Abuker Haji Hussein, director of the Somali Benadiri Community of Minnesota.

Although many different paths brought people to the state, in truth the unskilled workers who found jobs in

Marshall and then loudly blew a whistle were the greatest inspiration to Somalis who chose Minnesota for their new home. Thanks to the invaluable services, guidance, counseling, and, most of all, information the San Diego group passed on, the community members learned from each other. And as the Somali community has matured in number, evolved financially, and strengthened its roots in Minnesota, its members continue to share the same relevant details with new arrivals who find their way to the state today.

Religion

Somalis are 99.9, if not 100, percent Sunni Muslims who believe that their faith is the ultimate guiding principle of life. Their daily routines revolve around Islam's core teachings, which provide the rules for behavior in marriage, household management, financial gain, social interaction, attire, employment, raising children, and food consumption. To the Westerner the most conspicuous symbol of Muslim faith is the distinctive attire, specifically of women, as well as stopping all activity for prayer five times a day.[35]

Historically Somalis have been known to be moderate Sunnis. However, in the last thirty years or so religion itself has been weaponized in Somalia, first to resist Siad Barre's repressive regime, as in the late 1970s Somali women began to veil themselves for the first time. Second, during and after the civil war, Somali women became easy prey for sexual predators: crimes were rife in refugee camps and continue today. Justifiably, women used heavy clothing to hide their bodies from all ill-intentioned eyes.[36]

Five Pillars of Islam for Sunnis

Somalis who are Muslim Sunnis adhere to the five pillars of Islam. First, *Shahada* is declaring that God is the only God and that Muhammad is his messenger. Second, the faithful *pray* five times a day to their Creator. Third is the *zakat:* charitable giving to those who are in need. Fourth is *Ramadan,* during which the faithful fast from dawn to dusk for a whole month. And fifth is the *hajj* pilgrimage: if one is financially and physically able to travel, he or she must make at least one pilgrimage to Mecca to participate in prayer, ceremonies, and rituals.

From the early 1990s on, Islamic extremists, taking advantage of Somalia's political disintegration, began to import and then enforce strict religious interpretation onto society. Thus, a variation of women's veiling, known as *hijab, niqab, khimaar,* or *jilbaab,* replaced Somali women's traditional headdresses of *hagoog, garabasaar, masar, malkhabad, googarad, diric, garays,* and *guntiino* (the latter selection of words are all Somalized). The veil remains today for three reasons: first, in a not-so-safe world, Somali women feel protected by it, while at times they have used it to protest a repressive regime, as poet Nimo H. Farah attests:

> Her garments covered her scars
> And healed her battle wounds
> It is the Hijab that was her shield from fear
> The Hijab that was her security blanket as an infant
> Sentimental and Sacred.

Second, religious mercenaries have used the veil as a means of control. And third, a great number of Somali women adopted a variation of the veil as a distinct fashion statement and now own it as a marker of identity and pride. Farah also notes that a woman with a veil might have made the choice herself:

> She's brave with her ways but you want her to be free
> So that she can dance in your dreams
> You want to separate her body from her spirit
> Have one without the other
> She resists like the leaves resisting the wind.[37]

The Muslim lunar calendar is followed by all Muslims, and two major holidays are observed. Both are called *Eid.* One is right after the holy month of Ramadan, during which

Muslims fast from both food and drink from dawn to dusk. The end of that fasting is called the *Eid Ul Fitr,* meaning "breaking the fast" in Arabic. The other Eid is called *Adha,* when Muslims who are financially able perform the *hajj,* a pilgrimage to Mecca, in Saudi Arabia. Those who remain at home feast and pray in sympathy and union with those fortunate enough to make the journey. As for all people of Muslim faith, during these two major holidays wealthy Somalis offer the best charitable hand. Visiting is encouraged as family, friends, and relatives gather to eat, pray, and share what they have. Somalis cook their best meals and invite family and friends alike to share. Since the destruction of their nation, these two holidays also have become for Somalis a time of reaching out, as they call around the world in search of their separated loved ones, friends, colleagues, classmates, and neighbors to reconnect and remember. Fosiyo Mohamoud Ahmed, who lives in Minneapolis, said, "Both Eids take me to [an]other level. It feels like that I have endured and

---

Ramadan

Ramadan is the holy month that falls in the ninth month of the Islamic calendar based on the lunar year. During Ramadan, Muslims around the globe fast twenty-nine or thirty continuous days from dawn to dusk, meaning that the believer in Islam refrains from eating and drinking of any kind during those hours. The purpose is to teach the faithful about patience, submissiveness, and humility through spiritual journey. It is a time to reflect, atone, and feel for the neediest in the community: the sick, disabled, or poor. Ramadan moves backward by eleven days each year, thus falling behind the Georgian calendar.

Muslims around the globe break their fasting at sunset with a meal called *iftar,* first eating dates (three pieces, as their prophet Muhammad did). Then they perform their fourth round of daily prayer, followed by the optimum meal, enjoyed most when family and friends gather for a banquet of food and drink. Others converge on mosques, eating in communion, poor and rich sharing the meal together. At times large halls are reserved to serve the food to all who come. Besides the *zakat,* which is the obligatory Muslim duty of giving, *Sadaqa* (charity) is offered voluntarily. Muslims extend their giving hand during this time of year to reach the most vulnerable, the poorest, the sickest, and the neediest, including the homeless, the disabled, and their families, feeding, clothing, and comforting them.

been through a spiritual journey. I call all my friends, relatives, and family alike. As a matter of fact, I connect with people in Europe, Asia, Africa, and Australia as well, just to say 'hi.' It is a time of boundless cheer and bundle of joy because it is simply an Eid. The different kind of food, the conversation, the festive mood all around, and the get-together are all part of the celebration."[38]

Martisoor

Somalis are reaping the products of the civil rights movement, its seeds sown even before Somalia came into existence. Progressive figures such as Hubert Humphrey, who as vice president was the first high-ranking American official to visit Somalia, in January 1968; Walter Mondale; Eugene McCarthy; and Paul Wellstone, who in the 1990s kept that legacy alive by placing immigration issues on his political agenda, made it possible for the largest number of African refugees—Somalis—to be part of the Minnesota blend of today. Minnesotans' warm spirit and caring courtesy, known as "Minnesota nice," is acknowledged and appreciated by many Somalis. Mohamoud Ahmed Mohamed, employed at a grocery halal market in Minneapolis, stated, "I feel I am quite at home here. People are warm, friendly, broad-minded, and tolerant—should I go on? And, better yet, employment opportunities are much better here than anywhere else that I am aware of."[39]

Others lend support to this notion with their own experience. Hassan Ali Mohamed, who holds a master's degree in dental hygiene and now lives in Fridley with his family, said that his relocation to Minnesota was "deliberately calculated," for he had begun researching which state would offer him the best possible opportunity for raising a family, expanding his education, and finding a job that would pay the bills. Mohamed said,

I came to Phoenix, Arizona, in May of 1992, found a good job, registered for classes at a community college, and wanted to get established there. But the hot weather was unbearable, so I moved to Seattle, Washington. In Seattle, I thought to make it there I should rather be armed with an advanced degree. Both transportation and jobs were tough for people like me, an immigrant. Again I moved, this time to Kansas City, Missouri, and worked two janitorial jobs for $4.75 and $5.30 an hour each. I could not continue with that kind of financial strain . . . and could not see a way out for an immigrant like me either . . . For that reason, my move here was deliberately calculated. I looked into several better livability state indexes and concluded that Minnesota was at the top. The main reason for the relocation was for jobs. You could get the same job I had there here but with better wages . . . Now I am in much better shape than minimum wage, I tell you.[40]

Abdicadir Abucar Ga'al, who lives in Willmar with his family, stressed that Minnesotans went above and beyond the call of duty to see that Somalis were not the targets of misplaced anger during the time he calls the worst days to be a Muslim, as well as a Somali, in the United States: the days and months after September 11, 2001.

Listen, the people of Minnesota have not been given their due credit by the Somali community. I will never forget, right after September 11, living in Marshall, Minnesota, how the police would go out of their way to stop us in the middle of the street, asking whether anyone had bothered us. They repeatedly said to us, "Please let us know if you encounter any inappropriate comments or

mistreatment in any way or shape." I have to tell
you . . . hearing that from a police[man] in Middle
America made me believe in the people of this
state . . . All I am asking of myself and my family
is how can I contribute to that kind of common
humanity and inclusive attitude?[41]

Southeast Asians who resettled in Minnesota in the
1970s, mostly Vietnamese but also Cambodians, Laotians,

Abdicadir Abucar
Ga'al's family.
Left to right:
Weheliye Ga'al,
Ewni Ga'al,
Fowsiya Ga'al,
Abdullahi Awale,
Indhadeq Ga'al,
Marryan Ga'al,
and Lul Ga'al.

Thai, and Hmong—communities that share not only the hardship of war but other social similarities with Somalis—had put up ladders that helped lift the arriving Somalis twenty years later. For example, the social service providers and resettlement agencies had learned from the Hmong what material goods and supports were vital to new arrivals. Thus, as Somalis poured into Minnesota, these agencies either knew what to deliver and how, or, if they did not know, they had an idea of whom else to call.[42]

Fozia Adani, a teaching assistant in Minneapolis, shared her thoughts:

> I had friends who moved to Minneapolis. At the beginning, subsidized housing was much easier to get than in Tennessee, we were told. So I left my husband in Nashville and came to Minneapolis. Within two weeks, we moved into a two-bedroom apartment and my husband joined us a little later. I was already working when my husband came, and he got a job

---

Race Relations

Though examples of racism experienced by Somalis are limited overall, nettlesome incidents do surface here and there. A flare-up was reported in St. Cloud, for example, when epithet graffiti aimed at East Africans were painted on walls. In March 2010, the Council of American-Islamic Relations (CAIR) requested a federal investigation into allegations of harassment toward Muslim students of Somali origin in St. Cloud and Owatonna. The Justice Department's Civil Rights Division and the Department of Education's office have settled both cases. In the aftermath of 9/11, fears of retaliatory actions amounted to no more than verbal abuses aimed at women of Muslim faith, whose distinctive clothing makes them easily identifiable. Other examples of faith- or race-based incidents include Muslim men being refused a flight at the Minneapolis–St. Paul International Airport and Muslim employees filing discrimination complaints against employers. In November 2008, Somali poultry workers settled a discrimination lawsuit with Gold'n Plump, based in St. Cloud. In Rochester in the late 1990s and, more recently, in May 2012, "KKK" was painted on the home of a Somali American family. Thus, crude manifestations of racism exist, but they are not prevalent enough to deter Somalis from choosing to make Minnesota their new home.

in less than two weeks. I have to tell you though, if it had not been for the two friends who were ahead of us, we would have not been here. Over the phone, they told us about Minnesota and extended their hospitality to my family. Now we own our home and five of my seven children are proud Minnesotans.[43]

Minnesotans' unwavering hospitality has inspired Somalis to invest in the state and its future. Both the educated, who could have gotten jobs wherever they chose, and the undereducated, who came here to work at the processing plants, understood one thing early on: Minnesota offers them and their children the comfort of home away from home. Though of course, as with any refugee group, there have been some challenges and the occasional tinge of racism, for the most part Somalis sense the social pulse of Minnesota's *martisoor* and its residents' inclusive tendencies, and they feel welcome.

Challenges

Despite Minnesota's welcoming communities, Somalis have faced challenges. A leading contender, experienced by immigrant groups over the centuries, involves proficiency in English, without which one cannot articulate his or her needs and air grievances. In a related issue, at the diaspora's peak, a housing shortage in Minneapolis brought forth unscrupulous landlords, who rushed to take advantage of the most vulnerable, preying on those with too many children, those who were not able to speak out or did not know their rights and were easily intimidated, and those who were simply tired of confrontations and unwilling to fight anymore. A study conducted by Katherine Fennelly of the University of Minnesota showed that, in 1996, "half of severely crowded households in the US were inhabited by immigrants." She continued, "immigrants are especially vulnerable because of barriers of language, large family size and concentration of ethnic enclaves. They are also particularly vulnerable to housing discrimination, either because they are unaware of their rights, or because they fear reprisals for reporting substandard conditions or exploits." Some landlords rented out uninhabitable units. Amina A. Barkadle, a Minneapolis resident, recounts,

It was hard to get around the conditions that the landlord would lay on you. They would ask rental history of one who had just arrived and never had any even in Somalia. So when I came to Minneapolis my brother and I moved into a place that was not asking any of that. It was a one-bedroom apartment in South Minneapolis. And of course it was a place that the landlord was not able to rent to anybody else: a dilapidated slum full of mice and cockroaches. It was not long before other relatives also arrived and soon there were five of us! We did so much scraping and cleaning. We succeeded in killing the cockroaches and some of the mice, too, with whatever poison we could find. But the mice died in all the wrong places, where we were not able to extract them. The bad smell would nauseate us for months and months. And even in that kind of an environment, the landlord was abusive and outright arrogant. I should add though, that this kind of atrocious treatment is still happening to low-income Somalis.[44]

At the other end of the spectrum were property owners who would not rent to Somalis at any price, denying them housing for dubious reasons—for example, that a family was too large or lacked a rental or reference history in the

United States. Considering the Somalis' most recent point of origin in refugee camps, such demands obviously went beyond what they could fulfill.[45]

As the landlords' abuses soared, Project 504, a nonprofit tenants' advocate agency created by two young Minnesotans, Gregory Luce, a lawyer, and Joan Resner, a social worker, for the sole purpose of assisting Somali Minnesotans, arrived at the scene. The two began a lonely court battle against predatory landlords while bringing the issue out into the open, with the tangible result of winning some of their cases. Their clients remember not only their legal advocacy but also their psychological support and even, in one instance, courageous carpentry delivered in the wee hours of a December night. Amal Abdi, who now lives in St. Paul, said,

> May God forever shower them with kindness. Greg and Joan were sent saviors. In December of 1998 the condition of the place we were paying rent to live in was unbearable. At least, however, I knew one thing, that the landlord was mistreating me and my children, so I refused to pay the rent. Then about 10:00 PM one night in December, the landlord walked in, took off a window in the living room, and walked out with it. I thought my six children and I were going to freeze to death. In panic I called a relative of mine in town but to no avail. He did not even have the decency to answer the phone. In despair, I finally gathered the courage to call Greg, who came flying in. My brother, I can tell you, this great man was there up until 2:30 AM boarding my windows. How can I ever pay him back just for that alone?

One of Abdi's oldest sons is now enrolled at Stanford University.[46]

The tragedy of September 11, 2001, brought gloom and fear into the Somali community: gloom, because Somalis, as they grieved with the rest of the nation, were acutely aware that those responsible for the attacks shared names and a religious faith with them; fear, because they worried about a backlash. So too, the horror of the event brought back cruel memories of the senseless destruction that had delivered pain to their families and others in their homeland. The negative fallout did not rise to the level Somalis feared, but it did yield intrusive probes within the community from the Federal Bureau of Investigation, which put pressure on the Somali money-wiring agencies by closing some (the most prominent, Al-Barakat, among them) and tightening the regulation rope on the rest. In addition, the scrutiny and investigations continued, at times reaching customers who sent large sums of money back to their families in Somalia. Community members felt the federal agency's weight, and the aggressive questioning alienated and angered a large number of them.

Of special note were investigations into the Somali money-wiring agencies, known as *hawala*. The hawala serve as a lifeline between the diaspora and the needy ones back home. It was initially—and erroneously—suspected that the September 11 hijackers had used money-wiring agencies to finance their scheme. As a result, Al-Barakat— Somalia's largest money-wiring agency, with an annual income of $140 million, which operates in forty countries and is the largest employer in Somalia—fell victim to those unfounded suspicions. Al-Barakat's assets around the world were frozen, and though the agency has yet to be proven guilty of any crime, its millions remain so.[47]

At present, the hawala agencies have not recovered from these injuries and have become perennial victims of "guilt by association" each time a new incident of terrorism erupts somewhere around the globe. One by one, all

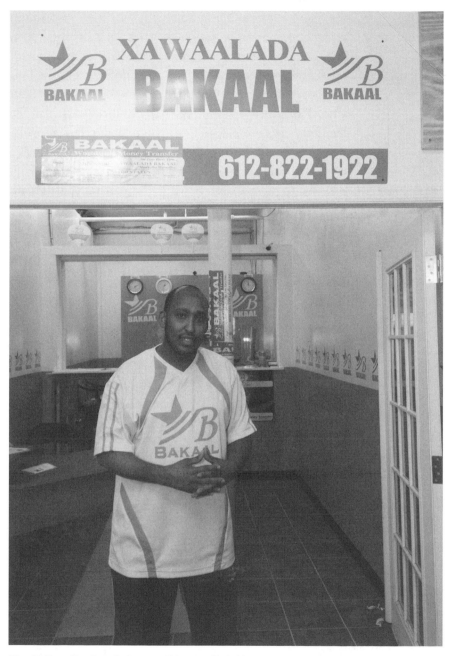

Liban M. Hussein, a Somalia-language TV personality in Minneapolis, has also jumped into the pool of money wiring. His hawala agency is boldly festooned with the company's name, Bakaal.

the major banks in Minnesota withdrew their association with Somalis' money-wiring agencies. One small outpost, Sunrise Community Banks, continued its relationship with the hawala, but, concerned about inquiries from the federal government, in December 2012 it, too, severed its relationship with the hawala agencies. Ironically, without the legitimacy of the U.S. banking system, dollars leaving Minnesota may unintentionally find their way into the hands of terrorists, such as al-Shabaab. Thousands of Somalis who have made their homes in Minnesota are galvanized and worried sick, wondering how they will feed the hungry back in Somalia without the lifeline of the hawala.

Social and School Interactions

With Somalis' arrival in Minnesota, cultural collisions soon surfaced in schools. In the 1990s, tensions began to rise in inner-city public schools, particularly at Roosevelt High in South Minneapolis, which at the time accommodated the largest number of Somali students. Conflict arose as African American students and Somali students, often in competition for the same limited resources, began fighting each other. These schoolyard challenges reflected what was happening in the adult communities, where families living in economically disadvantaged neighborhoods vied for inexpensive and subsidized housing, welfare and medical benefits, and other meager resources. Cultural collisions clouded cordial commonalities, and lack of a common language closed off communication channels that would have helped alleviate the pressure. Saeed Fahia, executive director of Confederation of Somali Community in Minne-

Charter Schools

In Minnesota, the birthplace of charter schools, Somalis are creating their own. At least ten charter schools are run by Somalis and populated by a Somali student body. And though their history is short, the schools continue to grow in number as well as in stature, with a promising future. One school to watch is Ubah Medical Academy, a high school in Hopkins.

sota, one of the leaders who had a mediating role, said, "We met on several occasions [with African American leaders], and concluded that the core of the conflict was mostly based on cultural and language miscommunications."[48]

Children naturally feel the stress and pressure affecting their parents; Somali students, struggling to fit into their adopted homeland and trying to learn a new language, resorted to physical confrontation when under verbal siege. Their opponents were most often African American students. That these two populations were packed into an economically deprived part of the inner city, riding the same bus lines, attending the same schools—all exacerbated the cultural misunderstandings.

Minneapolis was not alone in these confrontations, however: in Boston, Columbus, and San Diego, Somalis and African Americans collided. Some would argue that such conflict is part of the adaptation process, undergone by other populations and communities, including Polish, Irish, Italian, Jewish, and Scottish immigrants, over the decades.[49]

Mohamed
Abdullahi, the
city's first Somali
police officer,
on duty in South
Minneapolis.

Principals, teachers, writers, and conscientious community members on both sides tried to douse the fire of mis-
understanding with the conventional wisdom of learning
from and about each other. In the end, however, "it was the
student body that took the mantel away from everybody. It
was the student body that explored common causes, similarities, and searched ways to understand each other and
communicate better," said Saeed Fahia. "Once Somalis
learned the language, they began to handle themselves better verbally, found commonalities with their African American counterparts. And," he added, "in the most recent days
it seemed all that commotion between the two groups faded
away in the shadow of a distant past."[50]

One tragic outcome of these turf wars, however, helped
to foster Somali gangs, as young men who had partaken
in the earliest neighborhood and school fights were soon

battle groomed and toughened up, ready to take their fights to the streets. Erin Carlyle, writing for *City Pages,* described the shift: "As the clique grew, some of the new members . . . started getting into trouble—stealing cars or committing robberies. Before long the community began to regard them as a gang." Then they "became a state-documented gang after five of them were involved with the robbing and killing of a Somali woman." It is not surprising that the newly formed Somali street gangs soon turned on each other, vying for turf, recognition, and respect among their peers. And, as some of these young men aged with few skills other than fighting, the gangs took a criminal turn. One group is alleged to have developed into a prostitution ring, eventually spreading across state lines. Thirty suspects were indicted, bringing nationwide media attention to Minnesota. And though the federal investigation has been ongoing since 2007, so far only ten suspects have been brought to trial, with three proven guilty and seven released. The rest of the matter remains unresolved, but the community has been engulfed in a cloud of suspicion.[51]

Misguided Religious Passion

Cultural and religious misunderstandings were problematic for the adult Somali community at the same time that their children were struggling. One example hit the news in the summer of 2006, when a few ill-informed Somali airport taxi drivers, ignorant of both their religious obligations and the laws of the community, were accused of refusing to transport blind passengers and their guide dogs as well as passengers carrying alcohol. At these reports, Minnesota's Somalis engaged in lively debate: what did their religion dictate about staying away from both dogs and alcohol, and what did the law dictate about not allowing discrimination based on disability? Moderate groups spoke out against the drivers, as did Muslim clerics, while all concerned sought to appease and educate people both inside and outside the community.[52]

Then, shattering news shocked Minnesota's Somalis when, in October 2008, they woke to learn that one of their own, a naturalized U.S. citizen, had earned the dubious distinction of being the first American suicide bomber in Somalia. Shirwa Ahmed took his own life and the lives of thirty others in northwestern Somalia, in an area sometimes known as Somaliland. It soon followed that about twenty other young, impressionable, and vulnerable Somali males, all from the Minneapolis area, were either missing or known to already be in terrorist training camps or in the trenches with al-Shabaab, a radical al-Qaeda–affiliated Somali terror group. Al-Shabaab has come to be known for its brutality, stoning to death girls accused of adultery, chopping the hands of others accused of theft, and strapping young boys into suicide vests and sending them off to commit mayhem and mass murder.

Most of the young men were lured by the radical group after Ethiopia's army had marched through the Somali capital, Mogadishu, for the first time in the two countries' history. These men were either quite young when they had left Somalia or were raised in refugee camps or in America and did not remember much about what they and their families had run away from. Somalis and Ethiopians have been archenemies throughout their history, though in many ways the two peoples and countries are culturally similar. Now that Ethiopians had invaded Somalia under the pretext of fighting terrorists of what was then called the Islamic Courts—composed of religious groups, some of which later turned out to be al-Shabaab, which had taken control of most of southern Somalia in 2006—the group had a cause to call to arms: "liberating the nation." And these young men from Minnesota, facing some difficulties in their new home but also assured of a promising future, fell into the trap and ended up in al-Shabaab death camps.

The news caught the Somali community by surprise. Once again, clouds of suspicion brought questions about how some of their young men could have been approached by al-Shabaab and who financed their recruitment and travel. Underscoring that the community was feeling heated pressure from the FBI, the Minnesota chapter of the Council of American-Islamic Relations spoke out loudly. Professors Cawo Abdi and Abdi Samatar at the University of Minnesota also expressed their alarm and charged that the investigators were poorly informed.[53]

Fear that this home-grown threat could be used against the nation spurred the largest counterterrorism investigation since September 11, 2001, and brought about congressional hearings as well as once again putting the community under intense FBI scrutiny. The focus was on young Somalis in their teens or early twenties, in particular those who had attended Sanford Junior High as well as Roosevelt and Edison High, from which some of the young men who went to Somalia had graduated. Yearbook pictures in hand, the FBI would stop young Somalis at malls and in neighborhoods, often near the University of Minnesota campus. In South Minneapolis, pressure was also exerted onto Abubakar As-Saddique Islamic Center, which some of the young al-Shabaab recruits had frequented. After a thorough investigation, the center was cleared of any connection to the radical group.

In July 2011 Omar Mohamed Abdi, a twenty-six-year-old Somali American from Minnesota, pleaded guilty to providing material support to terrorists, admitting that he helped with the initial transportation of Somali men from Minnesota to Somalia in order for them to fight side by side with al-Shabaab. And then in October 2011, two Somali women from Rochester were among fourteen people federally indicted for aiding terrorists and collecting money to support al-Shabaab. They are now awaiting the possibility of very long sentences. The arrests, the fallout from the incriminating news, and anticipated corrective measures have burdened the community with collective, associative guilt.[54]

Entrepreneurial Spirit

Despite all the lost capital and business expertise that comes from uprooting one's life, Somalis' entrepreneurial spirit lives on, adjusting to new environments as it always has. One positive impression Somalis have long given the outside world relates to their fiercely independent streak. That same mind-set can be bent to the entrepreneurial sphere. When Somalis began arriving in a desolate, deserted part of Africa to shelter with other East African refugees, the women had, within days, set up businesses to sell items of interest, confronting the crisis of need head-on in order to feed their families.[55]

That independent streak is on display in Minnesota more so than anywhere else in the Western Hemisphere. According to Swedish economic historian Benny Carlson, who compares Somali communities in Sweden and Minnesota, "Minnesota offered an attractive environment that triggered off an influx of hard workers and daring

Saluma Omar in her jewelry shop, open for business at Karmel Mall.

entrepreneurs." Somalis, though here less than two decades, are conspicuously perched in many enterprises throughout Minneapolis—in grocery stores, halal meat shops, tea and coffee shops, restaurants, offices, community-run organizations, and, most of all, retail shops at malls. With characteristic independence combined with strong business acumen, Somalis saw an opportunity in their growing purchasing power and sought to capture it in several locations.[56]

One of hundreds of small clothing shops in Karmel Mall in South Minneapolis, displaying colorful skirts, blouses, *khimaar, hijab, diric,* and even oriental rugs.

The Phillips neighborhood of South Minneapolis, which has seen its share of economic distress, presents encouraging signs of Somalis' contributions. Formerly failing properties have been renovated to attract tenants, a significant number of them Somalis. On Franklin, Nicollet, and Cedar avenues, through the Cedar-Riverside area, and on Lake Street as well as throughout other sections of the metropolitan area are vibrant, Somali-owned and -operated businesses. Rehabilitated warehouses that

once stood empty in the middle of neighborhoods are now small Somali malls, villages within a city, brimming with over nine hundred business choices, humming with commerce.[57]

The overwhelming majority of these businesses generated their seed capital from a familial network that does not delay nor dictate payment terms. Inspired to start up a business, the entrepreneur consults with an individual in the nuclear family or from the larger clan network. The capital is then pooled and a business is built from the ground up. When that business succeeds, the original partners split, usually into smaller units, aiming to grow independent of each other to increase the profit margin. In most cases this splitting continues until each original collaborator reaches the ultimate goal of a solo ownership. Then, it is customary, "a call to duty" of sorts, that Somali business owners hire employees from within family or clan first—though a number of entities neither apply this nepotistic norm nor need to. Only then can other Somalis gain access to the dream of fortune through employment or paying a share. Thus, unlike most start-up businesses in the United States, most Somalis do not seek loans from conventional lenders, though a few are now using the African Development Center, a non-profit organization offering financial literacy training and

Afro Deli & Coffee

Afro Deli & Coffee, one of the most recent Somali-owned businesses to enter the food service arena in Minneapolis, opened its doors in January 2011 and holds the distinction of being the fastest to cross over to the mainstream population. Nestled in the African Development Center on the corner of Nineteenth Avenue South and Riverside, Afro Deli & Coffee is located in just the right place, close to the west bank area of the University of Minnesota and a short distance from Augsburg College, the University of Minnesota Medical Center, Health Partners Clinic, and the Cedar-Riverside neighborhood. It has become a favorite spot to get a bite of Somali, African, Mediterranean, and American food at a reasonable price.

Afro Deli & Coffee is owned and managed by a man with vision and passion, Abdirahman Issa Kahin. Kahin attributes his success to a dedication to service and to the deli's design, location, and good food. His plan: to ensure that African cuisine has its rightful share of the American market. "My goal is to develop this business into a franchise that is in league with Chipotle and the like. I will have fifty restaurants in ten years," he asserts.

Abdirahman Issa Kahin, owner of Afro Deli & Coffee.

more to amateur entrepreneurs. This practice of family financing has saved time and money, as business owners are not tethered with loads of loan interest or constricting conditions.[58]

One of the few Somali-owned businesses that prides itself in employing people based on qualifications, hard work, and reliability is a blend of a halal market and a bakery, called a *Durdur*. The name itself carries significant weight in Somali, meaning a continual stream of good fortune or a stream of clean water. These businesses are owned by an eclectic group of Somalis who share no specific clan affiliation. Besides the Somali name, a Durdur is defined as a business that owns its building outright and that has an identified management style with a hierarchal structure.

Other businesses operate in the American mainstream and are run by professionals. Gargar Clinic, for example, is an urgent care facility in Minneapolis that began operation in January 2011. In just a short span of time, Gargar has become a successful clinic, providing invaluable service to Somalis. The clinic is the first in the United States to be run exclusively by Somalis, and it is the first to take a Somali name, meaning "urgent care." At the helm is one of the most prominent, highly qualified Somali physicians, internist Dr. Mohamud Afgarshe, who also collaborates with a Hmong partner for an urgent care clinic in St. Paul.

Axis Medical Center is another Minneapolis clinic that in 2008 opened its doors primarily to Somalis. Though initially founded by a group of health care professionals including Somalis, it owes its notoriety and increased traffic to Dr. Abdirahman Mohamed, a passionate Somali family physician who came on board a year later. Dr. Mohamed has lived up to expectations by showing quality leadership and has served his community not only with the stethoscope.

Somalis' concept of seeing a physician and explaining their illness is different from that of the Western World. Therefore, a heavy burden is already off the shoulders of Somali patients once a Somali-speaking physician greets them. Then, patients feel at liberty to tell a long story about what they think is wrong; trust is immediately at a high level; and the feeling that they have been heard and understood puts them in a comfort zone that allows physician and patient to concentrate on healing.

Somalis are also, it seems, finding a bridge between the traditional financial world that they knew nothing about and the world that in turn knew nothing about them, including their clan system of financing. The African Development Center (ADC), a nonprofit alternative micro-financing organization run by Hussein Samatar, a Somali himself, offers small loan opportunities and training on financial literacy. Beyond assisting amateur entrepreneurs and aspiring businesspeople, ADC offers first-time home buyers the necessary knowledge to maintain their property. Traditional lenders, such as major banks, would ask for equity, credit history, a stable job, a cosigner, and a list of other requirements to which an immigrant, especially a Somali, might not have easy access. As ADC fills this void, it also serves a wider community—all Africans in Minnesota—but Somalis in particular identify with the organization and are easily able to communicate with its representatives. Thus, a great number of ADC's patrons are Somalis, who see ways to meet the needs of the community and have the characteristic initiative to open businesses as varied as their owners.[59]

The capital means as well as the financial seed generated by Somalis in Minnesota is palpably present as far back as East Africa or wherever Somalis are nowadays. The light of hope is bright and the entrepreneurial lessons bring pride. Somalis in Minnesota are not only conspicuously courageous in their business dealings but are also inspiring other eager minds.

Politics

By nature, a Somali is a political animal. Somalis' political participation on both the state and the federal level has been quite pronounced. A large share of the credit goes to the late Senator Paul Wellstone, who in the mid-nineties first approached the Somali community asking for votes while offering his profound capacity to show care and understanding. As a result, Somalis became active and informed members of the voting public. During his last campaign, while running for his third senatorial term in October 2002, Senator Wellstone came to the Somali community for an occasional candidate-meets-constituency gathering, where mundane demands were put to him. But nothing was mundane about how the senator responded to these questions. He made history by answering *haa*, or "yes" in Somali, when applicable.

Other politicians soon courted Somali votes or invited the community into the process. Republican Senator Norm Coleman was the first to hire a Somali staff member at the federal level, and he took pains to be well informed about Somalia's saga. Somalis have often found themselves aligned with the Democratic Party and in recent election cycles have feverishly campaigned for Congressman Keith Ellison, Senators Amy Klobuchar and Al Franken, Minneapolis Mayor R. T. Rybak, Governor Mark Dayton, and President Barack Obama. In 2010, Somalis in Minnesota made their own history when the first Somali American, Hussein M. Samatar, won a seat on the Minneapolis School Board. It is only a matter of time before other Somali Americans are elected to serve the larger community as well.[60]

Disputable Numbers

The Somali community in Minnesota is young enough that demographic information about it and its members remains anemic. Though there are no collected data on educational achievement and graduation rates specific to Somalis, anecdotal evidence is encouraging. Somalis are in classrooms at every educational level from kindergarten to college, including students pursuing advanced and doctoral degrees. Members of the first generation of Somali American postgraduates have already taken their places among the American workforce. An upward trend in educational achievement can be spotted in the medical students and those who have already passed the medical board examination as well as in the Somali students conspicuously present throughout the Minnesota State Colleges and Universities system. At the University of Minnesota in the Twin Cities, where the largest group of Somalis is enrolled, 280 to 350 Somali students attended in academic year 2011–12.[61]

Somalis' relative level of success in the employment arena is very difficult to measure from an academic point of view. Whatever scant information one can scrape together is unreliable. For example, one study shows the rate of employment among Somali males in Minnesota to be 65 percent, while another attests to a rate of 60 percent. One study indicates that 51 percent of the Somali population in Minnesota is living in poverty, while another brings the poverty level to 83 percent. It is difficult to gather employment information about Somalis because no category captures their net data from the larger pool of other Africans, blacks, people of African descent, and even other Muslims. This problem is compounded by the lack of trained eyes that, having gained the community's trust, could make accurate tracking possible. But one thing is quite clear: Somalis know they are doing better in Minnesota because of the strong jobs market and the increased business opportunities that come with it. This understanding brings confidence to the community, no matter how the numbers appear on a chart.[62]

A solid bearing on the number of Somalis living in the state of Minnesota has been elusive, too. Reasons for this uncertainty are many, but chief among them is that Somalis have long been suspicious of census takers, for in the past clans understood that power lay in numbers, and none would claim to be from a smaller group. In the United States, Somalis may be hesitant to enumerate who and how many are living at a particular address, fearing landlords may use the information against them. Second, during Siad Barre's repressive regime, a smaller population meant fewer resources would be allocated to that group. Today in the United States, no organization or entity is collecting data about this community. But the state of Minnesota is in good company: both Canada and the United Kingdom are in the same guessing boat. Canada estimates its Somali population to be between 35,000 and 200,000, and the United Kingdom offers estimates of between 44,000 and 250,000. The census of 2000 placed the number of Somalis in Minnesota at 11,164, but the community believes that number was impossibly low. Figures of 50, 60, 70, and even 80,000 have been tossed around. The latest derivative data from the 2010 census analysis estimated that about 36,000 Somalis live in Minnesota, but the community places that figure at 70,000. As the community continues to grow and as census categories are refined, firmer numbers will be at hand. Regardless of the inscrutable figures, however, Somalis in Minnesota are a visible minority whose members are thriving in business, are politically aware, and are patiently pursuing progress.[63]

Somalis as Minnesotans: Small Somalia

> "Immigrants are fairly mobile and move about freely, eventually settling where they have family, friends and/or a job."
>
> JUDY STUTHMAN, CHAIR, IMMIGRATION
> STUDY COMMITTEE OF THE LEAGUE OF
> WOMEN VOTERS OF MINNESOTA

Though the Minnesota Department of Human Services has zero entries for Somalis in Minnesota in 1992, the State Demographic Center states, "6 Somalis immigrated." A League of Women Voters study reports that there were two families, and sources for this book asserted that in the first half of the same year there might have been eighteen or fewer Somalis in Minneapolis, mostly self-supporting students. The following year, 1993, the Minnesota Department of Human Services, which keeps immigrant entry data, shows direct arrivals of 121 out of 2,753 nationwide. The figure dipped in 1994 to 73, rising to just below 600 in 1996, and then nearly tripling by 1999. Suddenly, according to the 2000 census, the number of Somalis in Minnesota was 11,164, a count that may in fact have been dismally low. The Somali community put the count at about 70,000, with an overwhelming majority residing in Minneapolis. But Somalis also have increasingly been moving on to other areas, such as Apple Valley, Burnsville, Eden Prairie, Edina, Fridley, Plymouth, Richfield, and St. Paul. Outside of the metro area, Somalis are still in Marshall as well as in Owatonna, Pelican Rapids, Rochester, St. Cloud, St. Peter, and Willmar. And of course, though the community has been growing in size and number, some members have been leaving Minnesota for other areas of the nation and world. Still, Minnesota, particularly Minneapolis, feels like a small Somalia at times.[64]

From interviews and the available scholarly work, it is evident that the largest number of Somali immigrants to

Table 2

YEAR	NUMBER OF SOMALI REFUGEES
1991	0
1992	0
1993	121
1994	73
1995	281
1996	538
1997	230
1998	287
1999	1,452
2000	1,964
2001	1,320

Source: Minnesota Department of Human Services

Minnesota came as a secondary wave. Once the first trickle arrived and people found jobs, the *war* spread like a wildfire. Somalis initially came to Minnesota because of employment opportunities in positions that did not require particular skills and language fluency. But Somalis stayed because they found Minnesota's hospitality to be durable, similar to their own *martisoor*. Resettlement assistance from social service agencies made them feel welcome. Minnesota further offers a strong set of economic assistance benefits that help refugees begin their new lives. And Somalis have established their own Minnesota identity, which is now an attraction in itself, also creating their own social service agencies to offer basic but essential assistance.[65]

People who survived refugee camps—now taxi drivers, hotel maids, janitors, teachers, business owners—see their children graduating from colleges, navigating the system like other Americans, and speaking English with an American accent, and they are proud of them. They came, they seized, and they settled. Somalis came to Minnesota when the *war* about the vibrant job market reached them, they seized the opportunity when *sahan* confirmed it, and they settled here when Minnesotans offered them *martisoor*. "You betcha," they are part and parcel of Minnesota now.

Personal Account: Mohamoud Bile Jama

An embodiment of those Somalis who have not felt resettled in the United States until they came to Minnesota is an immeasurably tenacious, determined, and resolved father of seven, Mohamoud Bile Jama, who shares his story, which like so many immigrant tales focuses on maximizing opportunity in unfamiliar territory.

Mohamoud was one of thirty-three refugees, a group of Somalis and Oromos, all originally from Ethiopia, who arrived in New York on March 6, 1989. Mohamoud, his pregnant wife, and three children were one of three Somali families heading to Fort Worth, Texas. After some struggles in Fort Worth and then Dallas, one day Mohamoud was at the post office to report a change of address when there, right before his eyes, stood a Somali man whom he had known back home in Mogadishu. After a huge healing hug, they began to catch up on each other's lives. The man recommended San Diego, California, with its burgeoning Somali community, as a new destination for Mohamoud's family.

Once there, they were welcomed with warm hearts and open arms. A Somali family shared a two-bedroom apartment with them. Gratefully, the family settled in, then rented a house, and slowly built a life. As more Somalis arrived, the neighborhood rapidly grew, but Mohamoud felt that progress remained slow. Wanting to invest in his children and their futures, he got on the phone with inquiries *(war/warraysi)* about employment prospects in other states and soon narrowed them down to two cities: Minneapolis, Minnesota, and Kansas City, Missouri.

Eventually he filled the tank of the family van and, with his recently graduated daughter and sixteen-year-old son in tow, left San Diego. He assessed both cities and then his Somali source of *war* led him to Rochester, Minnesota, where there were jobs. But what kind? He did not ask, nor did he care. He immediately went to the IBM building, where both he and his daughter filled out employment applications. They were hired on the spot for assembly work. Mohamoud asked his daughter's supervisor to allow her to wear her *hijab* on the job. He knew that some Somalis had been too timid to make this request. Thus, his daughter was the first to wear *hijab,* and soon the rest of the women followed. His sixteen-year-old son got a housekeeping job that same day and in fact began working while his sister and father were still going through the screening process at IBM. Mohamoud states:

> When time had come to relocate the whole family from San Diego to Rochester, Minnesota, I had to borrow the money to finance the trip although three family members were now working. I called a friend of mine and asked for a loan of three thousand dollars. I told him that I would pay him back in three months. He gave me the loan and I rented a U-Haul, sharing the rental cost with another family moving to Minnesota. In Minnesota I got my family under one roof and in three months paid off my friend. I was also able to repay another man who had sold me the van we drove to Minnesota on credit.
>
> While at IBM, I had asked that I work two shifts. Putting in many hours, I was able to save a little money. I was eventually laid off but was soon hired by another company that was very good to me and flexible enough to allow time off for Friday prayers.
>
> Then September 11, 2001, happened. That dreadful day I was at work but shortly thereafter I was laid off again.
>
> After six months of unemployment, it simply dawned on me that I had been chasing jobs that were out of my league. There and then, I decided to look for jobs that met my qualifications: lower-end jobs, janitorial, and the like. I put together a few dollars, telling people to invest with me, and became a janitorial subcontractor in two separate deals. As I expected, one of the two went under. The other, a carpet cleaning service, survived. We went on for five years. I had borne the obligation of caring for my family just fine.
>
> Once again I had plateaued. I did not want my children to be indebted to a life of cleaning dirt, nor did I want them to see me toiling. I needed to make a change if I was going to continue my climb up the ladder. I had been eyeing a business [a combined halal grocery and a Somali bakery, the first of its kind] where I had been both a customer and service provider. I had been telling the guys who owned it that they needed me. Lo and behold

Mohamoud Bile Jama, one of the owners of Durdur.

a share of the business was for sale. I was able to scrape together half of the money, mainly from my oldest daughter and son. I gave the guys my word that I was going to come up with the other half within a year. Luckily they acceded to my plea. A year later, once more with the help of my two oldest children, Fozia and Mohamed, I came up with remainder of the money for the share.

Today, I have three college graduates—Ramla, Hodan, and Mohamed, all from the University of Minnesota; Abdinasir is a student at the University of Minnesota as we speak, Hamza is studying at a community college on his way to a four-year college, and the youngest, Salma, is already college bound, hoping to attend the University of Minnesota, too; and Fozia, the oldest, has an associate of arts degree, with a plan towards her bachelor's degree. I own two businesses and a house in Apple Valley. *Alhamdu lilaha,* I am blessed.

Mohamoud Bile Jama speaks very modestly here, but he is a successful businessman in Minneapolis who beams with pride that all of his children have achieved or are on the path to what his parents were not able to give him: a college education.[66]

Further Reading

Andrzejewski, B. W., and Sheila Andrzejewski. *An Anthology of Somali Poetry.* Bloomington: Indiana University Press, 1993.

Cassanelli, Lee V. *The Shaping of Somali Society: Reconstructing the History of a Pastoral People, 1600–1900.* Philadelphia: University of Pennsylvania Press, 1982.

Gaildon, Mahmood. *The Yibir of Las Burgabo.* Trenton, NJ: Red Sea Press, 2005.

Hanley, Gerald. *Warriors: Life and Death Among the Somalis.* London: England, 1993.

Kapteijns, Lidwien, and Maryan Omar Ali. *Women's Voices in a Man's World: Women and the Pastoral Tradition in Northern Somali Orature, c. 1899–1980.* Portsmouth, NH: Heinemann, 1999.

Laitin, David D. *Language Repertoires and State Construction in Africa.* Cambridge: Cambridge University Press, 1992.

Laurence, Margaret. *A Tree for Poverty: Somali Poetry and Prose.* Toronto: ECW Press, 1993.

Lewis, I. M. *A Modern History of the Somali: Nation and State in the Horn of Africa.* Oxford: James Currey, 2002.

———. *A Pastoral Democracy: A Study of Pastoralism and Politics Among the Northern Somali of the Horn of Africa.* London: Published for the International African Institute by the Oxford University Press, 1967.

Mohamed, Nadifa. *Black Mamba Boy.* Hammersmith, London: Harper Collins, 2010.

Samatar, Abdi Ismail. *The State and Rural Transformation in Northern Somalia, 1884–1986.* Madison: University of Wisconsin Press, 1989.

Samatar, Ahmed I. *Socialist Somalia: Rhetoric and Reality.* London: Institute for African Alternatives, 1988.

Samatar, Said S. *Oral Poetry and Somali Nationalism: The Case of Sayyid Maḥammad 'Abdille Ḥasan.* Cambridge: Cambridge University Press, 1982.

Notes

1. Scores of scholars have voiced dissatisfaction with the paucity of available information on the Somalis in the areas of archeology, language, ethnography, and anthropology. See Ahmed I. Samar, *Socialist Somalia: Rhetoric and Reality* (London: Institute for African Alternatives, 1980), 9; Lee V. Cassanelli, *The Shaping of Somali Society: Reconstructing the History of a Pastoral People, 1600–1900* (Philadelphia: University of Pennsylvania Press, 1982), 4; David D. Laitin and Said S. Samatar, *Somalia: Nation in Search of a State* (Boulder, CO: Westview Press, 1987), 4.

Somaale, the incorrect spelling of *Soomaale*—propagated by non-Somali-speaking scholars prior to introduction of the Somali orthography and wrongly accepted by Somali-speaking scholars—is the etymological origin of *Soomaali* in the Somali language or *Somali* in English (others also say the word is *Samaale*). The spelling I prefer to use is *Soomaale.* Soomaale was the mythical patriarchal figure who, it has been said, fathered four out of the six largest Somali clans. Hence Daarood, Isaaq, Dir, and Hawiye of Soomaale descendants are today called Somalis. The other two are Mirifle and Digil of Rahanwayn. This ancestral claim has been lent credibility by I. M. Lewis: *Understanding Somalia and Somaliland Culture, History, Society* (London: Hurst & Co, 2008).

2. Abdi Ismail Samatar and Ahmed I. Samatar, "Somalis as Africa's First Democracy: Premier Abdirizak H. Hussein and President Aden A. Osman," *Bildhaan: An International Journal of Somali Studies* 2.1 (2002): 1–64; Samar, *Socialist Somalia,* 60.

3. Ismail Ali Ismail. *Governance: The Scourge and Hope of Somalia* (Bloomington, IN: Trafford Publishing, 2010), 148.

4. Samatar and Samatar, "Somalis as Africa's First Democracy"; Theodore M. Vestal, *The Lion of Judah in the New World: Emperor Haile Selassie of Ethiopia and the Shaping of Americans' Attitudes Toward Africa* (Santa Barbara, CA: Praeger, 2011), 154; Ahmed Ismail Yusuf, unpublished paper, 1997.

5. David D. Laitin, *Language Repertoires and State Construction in Africa* (Cambridge: Cambridge University Press, 1992), 93.

6. Helen Chapin Metz, *Somalia: A Country Study* (Washington, DC: Federal Research Division, Library of Congress, 1993), 216; Donna R. Jackson, *Jimmy Carter and the Horn of Africa: Cold War Policy in Ethiopia and Somalia* (Jefferson, NC: McFarland & Co, 2007).

7. Jeffrey Alan Lefebvre, *Arms for the Horn: U.S. Security Policy in Ethiopia and Somalia, 1953–1991* (Pittsburgh, PA: University of Pittsburgh Press, 1991).

8. Samar, *Socialist Somalia,* 138; Anna Simon, *Networks of Dissolution: Somalia Undone* (Boulder, CO: Westview Press, 1995), 49.

9. Dietrich Jung, *Shadow Globalization, Ethnic Conflicts and New Wars: A Political Economy of Intra-State War* (London: Routledge, 2003), 167; International Congress of Somali Studies, Jörg Janzen, and Stella von Vitzthum, *What Are*

Somalia's Development Perspectives? Science between Resignation and Hope? Proceedings of the 6th SSIA Congress, Berlin 6–9 December 1996. Berlin: Das Arabische Buch, 2001; Nuruddin Farah, *Yesterday, Tomorrow: Voices from the Somali Diaspora* (London: Cassell, 2000); Belachew Gebrewold-Tochalo, *Anatomy of Violence: Understanding the Systems of Conflict and Violence in Africa* (Farnham, Surrey: Ashgate, 2009), 133; Kidane Mengisteab and Cyril K. Daddieh, *State Building and Democratization in Africa: Faith, Hope, and Realities* (Westport, CT: Praeger, 1990).

10. Alice Bettis Hashim, *The Fallen State: Dissonance, Dictatorship, and Death in Somalia* (Lanham, MD: University Press of America, 1997), 31; Hussein Ali Dualeh, *Search for a New Somali Identity* (Nairobi: H. A. Dualeh, 2002); Donald A. Sylvan and James F. Voss, *Problem Representation in Foreign Policy Decision Making* (Cambridge: Cambridge University Press, 1998), 126; Anuradha Kumar, *Human Rights: Global Perspectives* (New Delhi: Sarup & Sons, 2002); Human Rights Watch, *Hostile Shores: Abuse and Refoulement of Asylum Seekers and Refugees in Yemen* (New York: The organization, 2009).

11. Hashii Abdinur Nur, *Weapons and Clan Politics in Somalia* (Mogadishu?: 1996); Aidan Hartley, *The Zanzibar Chest: A Story of Life, Love, and Death in Foreign Lands* (New York: Atlantic Monthly Press, 2003), 178.

12. Gary W. Boyd, *McGuire Air Force Base* (Charleston, SC: Arcadia, 2003), 8.

13. Jonathan Stevenson, *Losing Mogadishu: Testing U.S. Policy in Somalia* (Annapolis, MD: Naval Institute Press, 1995); Mohamed Diriye Abdullahi, *Culture and Customs of Somalia* (Westport, CT: Greenwood Press, 2001), 47.

14. Mark Bowden, *Black Hawk Down: A Story of Modern War* (New York: Atlantic Monthly Press, 1999); Jerry Bruckheimer, et al., *Black Hawk Down* (Culver City, CA: Columbia TriStar Home Entertainment, 2002).

15. C. M. A. Horst, *Money and Mobility: Transnational Livelihood Strategies of the Somali Diaspora,* Global Migration Perspectives 9 (Global Commission on International Migration, 2004), available: http://www.unhcr.org/refworld/country „GCIM„SOM„42ce49684,0.html.

16. Judish Gardner and Judy El-Bushra, *Somalia—The Untold Story: The War Through the Eyes of Somali Women* (London: CIIR, 2004), 66.

17. Farah, *Yesterday, Tomorrow,* 2, 5.

18. Abdikadir Jama, interview with the author, Mar. 20, 2012; Women's Rights Project and Human Rights Watch, *The Human Rights Watch Global Report on Women's Human Rights* (New York: The organization, 1995); Shoran Pickering, *Women, Borders, and Violence: Current Issues in Asylum, Forced Migration and Trafficking* (New York: Springer, 2011), 27, available: http://public.eblib.com/EBLPublic/PublicView.do?ptiID=770179.

19. Refugee Arrivals by Region and Country of Nationality, Department of Homeland Security, available: http://www.dhs.gov/files/statistics/publications/YrBk03RA.shtm; Abdi Husen, "A Nomad's Journey to Minnesota," *Twin Cities Daily Planet,* Nov. 25, 2009, available: http://www.tcdailyplanet.net/news/2009/11/25/nomads-journey-minnesota.

20. Husen, "A Nomad's Journey."

21. Abdikayd, interview with the author, Nov. 21, 2011.

22. Abdicadir Abucar Ga'al, interview with the author, July 2, 2011.

23. Carl Walsh, "What Caused the 1990–1991 Recession?" *Economic Review of the Federal Reserve Bank of San Francisco* 2 (1993): 34–48, available: http://www.frbsf.org/publications/economics/review/1993/93-2_34-48.pdf; "Where can I find the unemployment rate for previous years?" Bureau of Labor Statistics, available: http://www.bls.gov/cps/prev_yrs.htm; "Slaying the Dragon of Debt: Fiscal Politics and Policies from the 1970s to the Present," timeline, early 1990s recession, available: http://bancroft.berkeley.edu/ROHO/projects/debt/index.html.

24. Interviews with the author: Abdicadir Abucar Ga'al; Hassan Ali Mohamed, July 3, 2011.

25. Safiya Ahmed Dirir, interview with the author, July 19, 2011.

26. Abdi Husen, interview with the author, June 22, 2011.

27. Abdi Husen interview.

28. Abdicadir Abucar Ga'al interview.

29. Dr. Abdirahman D. Mohamed, interview with the author, Sept. 9, 2011.

30. Dr. Mohamed is also on a senior advisory board of the Bill and Melinda Gates Malaria Foundation that convenes monthly in Seattle.

31. Dr. Fozia Abrar, interview with the author, July 2, 2011.

32. Abdulla Mohamed, interview with the author, Sept. 21, 2011.

33. Mohamed Abuker Haji Hussein, interview with the author, June 7, 2012.

34. Abdi Mohamoud Suleiman, interview with the author, June 7, 2011.

35. Abdullahi, *Culture and Customs of Somalia,* 55.

36. Women's Rights Project and Human Rights Watch, *Global Report on Women's Human Rights;* Pickering, *Women, Borders, and Violence,* 27.

37. Cawo Abdi, "Convergence of Civil War and the Religious Right: Reimagining Somali Women," *Journal of Women in Culture and Society* 33.1 (2007); Heather Marie Akou, "Nationalism Without a Nation: Understanding the Dress of Somali Women in Minnesota," in *Fashioning Africa: Power and the Politics of Dress,* ed. Jean Marie Allman (Bloomington: Indiana University Press, 2004), 50–63; Bashir Goth, "Against the Saudization of Somaliland, Somaliland; II; III," *Somaliland Times,* n.d., available: http://www.somalilandtimes.net/2003/92/9219.shtml; Nimo H. Farah, e-mail to the author, Aug. 1, 2012.

38. Fosiyo M. Ahmed, interview with the author, Aug. 10, 2012.

39. Iric Nathanson, "'Into the Bright Sunshine': Hubert Humphrey's Civil-Rights Agenda," *MinnPost,* May 23, 2011, available: http://www.minnpost.com/politics-policy/2011/05/bright-sunshine-hubert-humphreys-civil-rights-agenda; Timothy Nels Thurber, *The Politics of Equality: Hubert H. Humphrey and the African American Freedom Struggle* (New York: Columbia University Press, 1999); Ihotu Ali, "Staying off the Bottom of the Melting Pot: Somali Refugees Respond to a Changing U.S. Immigration Climate," *Bildhaan: An International Journal of Somali Studies* 9.1 (2011): 89–114; Vestal, *Lion of Judah,* 154; Frank James, *The Two-Edged Sword* (Carmangay, Alberta: Saga Books, 2006), 125; Mohamoud Ahmed Mohamed, interview with the author, July 12, 2011.

40. Hassan Ali Mohamed, interview with the author, July 12, 2011.

41. Abdicadir Abucar Ga'al interview.

42. Elizabeth Dunbar, "Comparing the Somali Experience in Minnesota to Other

Immigrant Groups," Minnesota Public Radio, Jan. 22, 2010, available: http://minnesota.publicradio.org/display/web/2010/01/25/comparing-the-somali-experience-in-minnesota-to-other-immigrant-groups-of-immigrants-/.

43. Fozia Adani, interview with the author, June 20, 2011.

44. Katherine Fennelly, "Listening to the Experts: Provider Recommendations on the Health Needs of Immigrants and Refugees," 9, available: http://dspace.mah.se/handle/2043/688; Amina A. Barkadle, interview with the author, Aug. 2, 2012.

45. Steve Brandt, "Conflicts between Somalis, Some Landlords Are Growing," Minneapolis *Star Tribune,* June 22, 1998.

46. Paul Levy and staff writer, "Social Worker, Lawyer Put Lives on Hold to Help Somalis in Condemned Buildings," Minneapolis *Star Tribune*, June 2, 2000; Amal Abdi, interview with the author, Mar. 20, 2012.

47. Tatsha Robertson, "Somalis Decry Closing of Money Centers," *Boston Globe,* Nov. 9, 2001, A14.

48. Gladys Mambo, "Minnesota Youth News: It Ain't All about Race," Minneapolis *Star Tribune,* Jan. 15, 2001; Saeed Fahia, interview with the author, Aug. 11, 2012.

49. Kimberly Hayes Taylor and staff writer, "Somalis in America: Working through a Clash of Cultures," Minneapolis *Star Tribune*, Mar. 22, 1998.

50. Said Fahia, interview with the author, May 24, 2012; Rohan Preston and staff writer, "Conflict Resolution: For 'Snapshot Silhouette,' Her First Play Aimed at Younger Audiences, Kia Corthron Scopes Out Tension between Black and Somali Youth," Minneapolis *Star Tribune*, Mar. 19, 2004.

51. Erin Carlyle, "Minneapolis Somali Community Facing Dark Web of Murders," *City Pages,* Nov. 21, 2008, available: http://www.citypages.com/2008-11-12/news/minneapolis-somali-community-facing-dark-web-of-murders; David Chanen and James Walsh, "A Huge Web of Gang Crime: Sex Ring Was Part of Financial Network Far Beyond the Twin Cities," Minneapolis *Star Tribune,* Nov. 10, 2010.

52. Barbara Pinto, "Muslim Cab Drivers Refuse to Transport Alcohol, and Dogs," *ABC News,* June 20, 2007, available: http://abcnews.go.com/International/story?id=2827800&page=1#.UBwngfZlRcQ; Kamal Nawash, "Free Muslims Condemn Cab Drivers Who Refuse to Pick Up Passengers with Alcoholic Beverages," War to Mobilize Democracy, available: http://netwmd.com/blog/2006/10/15/1071.

53. David Johnston, "Militants Drew Recruit in U.S., F.B.I. Says," *New York Times,* Feb. 23, 2009, available: http://www.nytimes.com/2009/02/24/washington/24fbi.html; Laura Yuen, "Minnesota Men Join 'Jihad' in Somalia," Minnesota Public Radio, Nov. 2011, available: http://minnesota.publicradio.org/projects/ongoing/somali_timeline/missing_men2; Cawo M. Abdi, "The War on Terror, Somali Minnesotans—and Ill-Informed Investigators," *MinnPost,* Mar. 20, 2011, available: http://www.minnpost.com/community-voices/2009/03/war-terror-somali-minnesotans-and-ill-informed-investigators; "CAIR Moves to 'Prevent' Muslim Students from FBI Questioning," Apr. 10, 2009, available: http://www.newsnet14.com/?p=45075; "CAIR Invites FBI Director to Minneapolis Mosque," video, Feb. 24, 2009, available: http://www.unz.org/Pub/CAIRTV-2009-00017.

54. Carol Cratty, "Somali-American

Man Admits Helping Men Travel to Somalia to Fight," CNN, July 18, 2011, available: http://articles.cnn.com/2011-07-18/justice/minnesota.conspiracy.plea_1_al-shabaab-somali-government-troops-shirwa-ahmed?_s=PM:CRIME; Allie Shah and Rose French, "Rochester Women Guilty of Aiding Somali Terror Group," Minneapolis *Star Tribune,* Oct. 20, 2011, available: www.startribune.com/local/minneapolis/132239033.html.

55. James Harry Humphrey, *Issues in Contemporary Athletics* (New York: Nova Science Publishers, 2007), 21; Lewis, *Understanding Somalia,* 132.

56. Benny Carlson, "Hard Workers and Daring Entrepreneurs: Impressions from the Somali Enclave in Minneapolis," in *The Role of Diasporas in Peace, Democracy and Development in the Horn of Africa,* ed. by Ulf Johansson Dahre (Lund: Lund University, Departments of Sociology and Political Science, 2007), 184.

57. Hussein H. Samatar, "Experiences of Somali Entrepreneurs: New Evidence from the Twin Cities," *Bildhaan: An International Journal of Somali Studies* 10.1 (2010): 89–102.

58. Samatar, "Experiences of Somali Entrepreneurs," 78–91.

59. Ali, "Staying Off the Bottom of the Melting Pot."

60. Laura Yuen, "First Somali-American Elected to Public Office in Minnesota," Minnesota Public Radio, Nov. 3, 2010, available: http://minnesota.publicradio.org/display/web/2010/11/03/hussein-samatar-first-somali-american-to-hold-public-office-in-minnesota; Mattie Weiss, "Wellstone's Secret Weapons," available: http://nypolisci.org/files/poli16/Readings/Wellstones%20Secret%20Weapon-%20Mattie%20Weiss-%20pp%2085-96.pdf.

61. Zuhur Ahmed, interview with the author, Sept. 12, 2012.

62. Carlson, "Hard Workers and Daring Entrepreneurs "; Cawo M. Abdi, "The Newest African-Americans?: Somali Struggles for Belonging," *Bildhaan: An International Journal of Somali Studies* 11. 1 (2011): 90–107; Louise Dickson, "Revival of the Civil Spirit: Contradictions in Somali-American Citizenship," *Bildhaan: An International Journal of Somali Studies* 11. 1 (2011):109–21; Owen Truesdell, "*E Pluribus Unum*: 21st-Century Citizenship and the Somali-American Experience," *Bildhaan: An International Journal of Somali Studies* 11. 1 (2011): 22–134.

63. Renata D'aliesio, "Young Canadian-Somalis Drawn to Activism," *Saturday's Globe and Mail,* Sept. 23, 2011, available: http://www.theglobeandmail.com/news/national/toronto/globe-to/young-canadian-somalis-drawn-to-activism/article2178580/page1/; J. Stuthman, League of Women Voters of Minnesota, Immigration Study Committee, "The Largest Number of Somalis in the United States with Estimates Ranging from 20,000 to 50,000," available: http://www.diversitycouncil.org/PDF_files/immigrant_study_lwv.pdf; Denise Grady, "Foreign Ways and War Scars Test Hospital," *New York Times,* Mar. 28, 2009, available: http://www.nytimes.com/2009/03/29/health/29immig.html?_r=2&pagewa; Lewis, *Understanding Somalia;* Chris Wamalwa and Nick Oluoch, "Somali Diaspora Supports Incursion," *Ajabu! Weekly News for Africans Abroad,* Oct. 31, 2011; "Minnesota Continues to Have Largest Somali Population in the Nation," *Zebraic and Askew,* available: http://blog.lib.umn.edu/aske0036/3101newsfall2011/2011/11/minnesota-continues-to-have-largest-somali-population-

in-the-nation.html; "State's Somali Population Grows," Minneapolis *Star Tribune,* Oct. 28, 2011, available: http://www.startribune.com/local/132752328.html.

64. Barbara J. Ronningen, "Estimates of Selected Immigrant Populations in Minnesota, 2004," Minnesota State Demographics Center, June 2004, available: http://www.demography.state.mn.us/PopNotes/EvaluatingEstimates.pdf; U.S. Department of Homeland Security, "Yearbook of Immigration Statistics, 2003: Refugees and Asylees," available: http://www.dhs.gov/files/statistics/publications/YrBk03RA.shtm.

65. Ronningen, "Estimates of Selected Immigrant Populations "; Dianna Shandy and Katherine Fennelly, "A Comparison of the Integration Experiences of Two African Immigrant Populations in a Rural Community," *Journal of Religion & Spirituality in Social Work* 25.1 (2005): 23–45; Ali, "Staying Off the Bottom of the Melting Pot"; Stuthman, "Largest Number of Somalis"; Katherine Fennelly and Helga Lietner, "How the Food Processing Industry Is Diversifying Rural Minnesota," working paper, Julian Samora Research Institute (2002), available: http://www.jsri.msu.edu/pdfs/wp/wp59.pdf; Carlson, "Hard Workers and Daring Entrepreneurs," 184; K. Darboe, "New Immigrants in Minnesota: The Somali Immigration and Assimilation," *Journal of Developing Societies* 19.4 (2003): 458; Horst, *Money and Mobility.*

66. Mohamoud Bile Jama, interview with the author, Aug. 12, 2012.

Notes to Sidebars

i. Richard Dowden, *Africa: Altered States, Ordinary Miracles* (New York: Public Affairs, 2009), 92; Gerald Hanley, *Warriors: Life and Death Among the Somalis* (London: Eland, 2004), 29.

ii. Dowden, *Africa,* 92.

iii. Beverly Allen and Mary Russo, *Revisioning Italy National Identity and Global Culture* (Minneapolis: University of Minnesota Press, 1997), 141, available: http://public.eblib.com/EBLPublic/PublicView.do?ptiID=310410.

iv. Waris Dirie and Cathleen Miller, *Desert Flower: The Extraordinary Journey of a Desert Nomad* (New York: William Morrow, 1998).

v. B. W. Andrzejewski and Sheila Andrzejewski, *An Anthology of Somali Poetry* (Bloomington: Indiana University Press, 1993), 3; Ahmed Ismail Yusuf, "A Thorn in the Sole: Short Story," *Bildhaan: An International Journal of Somali Studies* 5.1 (2005): 54; Abdullahi Hassan Roble, *Silsiladda Guba: Guba Poems* (Stockholm: Scansom Publishers, 1999).

vi. Somalis' job walkouts have mostly been reported as prayer disputes, but these events are also about Somalis' assertive attitude: Peter Passi, "Heartland: 82 Lose Jobs," *Independent* BUS, Sept. 13, 1993; "World News Briefs; In Pay Protest, Somalis Barricade U.N. Buildings," *New York Times,* Jan. 15, 1995, available: http://www.nytimes.com/1995/01/15/world/world-news-briefs-in-pay-protest-somalis-barricade-un-buildings.html; Associated Press, "Company Agrees to

Give Employees Prayer Breaks," *Charleston Daily Mail*, Dec. 4, 1999; "Dell Workers Walk Off Job over Prayer Dispute," available: http://www.msnbc.msn.com/id/7160832/; Kirk Semple, "A Somali Influx Unsettles Latino Meatpackers," *New York Times*, Oct. 15, 2008, available: www.nytimes.com/2008/10/16/us/16immig.html?pagewanted=all;"Mosqueing the Workplace: 130 Muslim Workers Walk Off Job at Tyson Meat Plant Demanding Prayer Time," available: http://www.topix.com/forum/city/anderson-mo/T71BP2OUPEO59VLMS; "Seattle, WA: Somalis Suspended for Praying on Company Time," available: http://actforamericaomaha.com/seattle-wa-somalis-suspended-for-praying-on-company-time%E2%80%A66/; and Rima Tima Berns McGown, *Muslims in the Diaspora: The Somali Communities of London and Toronto* (Toronto: University of Toronto Press, 1999).

vii. Interviews with the author: Hiss Ahmed Ismail, July 25, 2011; Hodan Adan (pseudonym), July 26, 2011.

viii. Interviews with the author: Safiya Ahmed Dirir, June 10, 2011; Abdihakim Ugas Aden Hadis, Nov. 30, 2011.

ix. See "College of Liberal Arts: Nuruddin Farah," University of Minnesota, Dec. 2011, https://apps.cla.umn.edu/directory/profiles/nfarahha; "Department of Geography: Abdi Samatar," University of Minnesota, Dec. 2011, http://www.geog.umn.edu/people/profile.php?UID=samat001; "International Studies: Ahmed Samatar," *Macalester College*, Dec. 2011, http://www.macalester.edu/internationalstudies/samatar.html; "Department of Sociology: Cawo Abdi," University of Minnesota, Dec. 2011, http://www.soc.umn.edu/people/abdi_c.html.

x. June D. Holmquist, *They Chose Minnesota: A Survey of the State's Ethnic Groups* (St. Paul: Minnesota Historical Society Press, 1981), 329; J. Clare Mortensen, "United States Policy on Southeast Asian Refugees, 1976–1980," 2, available: http://www.hhh.umn.edu/img/assets/24592/US%20Policy%20on%20Southeast%20Asian%20Refugees,%201976-1980.pdf.

xi. Thurber, *Politics of Equality*; Walter F. Mondale and Dave Hage, *The Good Fight: A Life in Liberal Politics* (New York: Scribner, 2010).

xii. Mortensen, "United States Policy"; David W. Haines, *Refugees in America in the 1990s: A Reference Handbook* (Westport, CT: Greenwood Press, 1996), 13–14.

xiii. Isaac Geedi, interview with the author, Nov. 29, 2011.

Index

Page numbers in *italic* refer to pictures and captions. Page numbers such as "87n1" refer to notes, e.g., note 1 on page 87.

Settlement patterns: in 1990s, 4, 19–20, 24–25, 28–29, 64; in 2000s, 64; Cedar-Riverside neighborhood, 29, 49, 56; Phillips neighborhood, Minneapolis, 56; Somali Benadiris, 34; southwestern Minnesota, 21, 23, 30

al-Shabaab (terrorist organization), 48, 52–54

Sharmarke, Abdirashid Ali, 6, 8

Siyad, Amina, 14–15

Social services, 41–42, 65

Somali Action Alliance, 30

Somali Benadiri Community of Minnesota, 30, 34, *35*

Somali Democratic Movement, 12

Somali Mai Community of Minnesota, 30

Somali National Movement, 12

Somalia: about, 4, 6; alliance with Soviet Union, 8–10; assistance from U.K., 10; assistance from U.N., 12; assistance from U.S., 10, 13, 19; Barre era, 8–12, 18–19, 63; Benadiri, 34; boundary disputes with Ethiopia, 6, 8, 19; civil war (1990s), 12–14; civilian rebellions, 12; elected officials, 8; European colonial rule, 6; first refugees, 18–19; independence and nationhood, 6, 7; invasion of Ethiopia (1977), 9, 19; military coup d'état, 8, 10; Operation Restore Hope, 13; terrorist training camps, 52–53

Somalia Salvation Democratic Front, 10

Soomaale, mythical patriarch, 71n1

Soviet Union: alliance with Ethiopia, 10; alliance with Somalia, 8–10

Stuthman, Judy, 63

Suleiman, Abdi Mohamoud, 34–35

Sunni Muslims: charitable giving, 36, 38; five pillars of Islam, 36; *hajj,* 36, 38; holidays, 37–38; prayer, 36, 38; Ramadan, 36, 37–38; suicide bombers, 52–53; taxi drivers' misunderstandings, 51–52; women's clothing, 36–37

Sunrise Community Banks, 48

Ubah Medical Academy, Hopkins, 48

United Kingdom: financial assistance, 10; Somali population estimate, 63

United Nations: food assistance, 12

United Nations High Commissioner for Refugees, 28

United Somali Congress, 12

United States: arms and financial assistance, 10, 19; humanitarian assistance, 13, 19; military assistance, 13; Somali refugees, 19

University of Minnesota, 27, 62

Vestal, Theodore, 8

Volunteer agencies (VOLAGs), 19, 25–28, 42

War (news): described, 1–3; in Minnesota, 25–27, 30–31, 35, 65; in San Diego, 19–21, 27; unemployment statistics (1990s), 24–25

Waryaa Sayers, 2

Wellstone, Paul, 39, 61

Women: clothing, 36–37, 49, 67–68; medical professionals, 33; small businesses, 54–60

Yemen: Somali refugees, 18

Picture Credits

Map page iv by David Deis. Photo page 41 courtesy Ga'al family. All other photographs by Bill Jolitz.

Acknowledgments

Reading a fascinating article, "A Nomad's Journey to Minnesota" by Abdi Husen, which appeared in the *Twin Cities Daily Planet* on November 25, 2009, deeply touched a nerve in me. The article authentically represented a stark picture of how a Somali would behave, and this idea of "a nomad's journey" appealed to me more than I would have liked to admit. So, when two years later Professor Cawo Abdi of the University of Minnesota passed on the idea for this book to me, I essentially already had my outline. Then, in conversation with a socially conscientious poet, Ahmed Mohamed Mohmoud, and a lifelong nonprofit governmental organizations devotee, Aden Abdi Adar, the prologue came into focus.

First and foremost, thanks to Maggi Larson, whose eagle eyes made all my mistakes minor. I am more in awe of you than you know.

Next, I distribute trophies of thanks. First, to my illiterate mother, who back in Somalia is somewhere on a mountaintop with a herd of sheep and goats: she instilled in me the value of education. An equally prized trophy to two indomitable, wise, and generous women, Khadra Haji Farah (Dudu) and Maryan Haji Hassan Ahmed, and of course to their husbands (my cousins), Ali Hassan Muse and General Ahmed Jama Muse, who were always there for me when I needed them most. To academic advisor Diane Zannoni of Trinity College in Hartford, Connecticut, whose great mind and guidance led me through college. To Barbara Furbish, a college friend who is like a sister, who taught me how to behave around women in America. Much thanks to Dr. Abdikadir Jibril Dualeh, who handed me my first book to read here in America, and to Dr. Jerome Kroll, who read and commented on an early draft. Lastly, to my lovely wife, Saud Mohmood Ateyah, who has not only been caring for our son Sahan but has put up with my inexplicable hours of absence. Thanks, Honey.

At the Minnesota Historical Society Press, I extend my gratitude to managing editor Shannon Pennefeather, who has been a cheerleader throughout the process. A book is a team effort: my thanks also to press director Pam McClanahan, to editor in chief Ann Regan, and to those behind the book's sales, promotion, and publicity: Alison Aten, Mary Poggione, and Leslie Rask.

I am quite humbled and greatly appreciative of Mohamoud Bile Jama's storytelling gift and how he trusted me with his intimate family story when many others shied away. I thank Abdicadir Abucar Ga'al, who connected the dots that mattered the most when relating stories about Marshall, Minnesota. Thanks to the Sioux Falls librarians, in particular to Heather Stevenson; and to Anduin Wilhide, whose comments strengthened the manuscript.

Finally, my utmost appreciation is extended to the following people: Said Salah Ahmed, Anwar Mohamed Diriye, Seinab Jama, Sahra Ulay, Hiss Ahmed Ismail, Ahmed Jamac (Qaldan), Dr. Fozia Abrar, Dr. Sahra Jama, Omar Gurase, Mohamoud Ahmed Mohamed, Hassan Ali Mohamed, Isaaq Geedi, Abdulla Mohamed, Abdi M. Suleiman, Abdikayd, Syed Ahmed, Abdihakim Ugas Aden Hadis, Yasin Ugas Aden Hadis, Kadar

Ugas Aden Hadis, Aden Jibril Aden, Dr. Abdirhaman D. Mohamed, Dr. Mohamed Abdirahman Hassan, Ahmed Mohamed Mohmoud, Adan Abdi Adar, Mohamed A. Ahmed (Mohamed Yare), Fatuma Elmi, Said Fahiya, Abdikadir Jama (Asaso), Mohamed Abuker Haji Hussein, Amal Abdi, Abdirashid Warsame, Mohamud Mumin, Nimo H. Farah, Anina A. Barkadle, Zuhur H. Ahmed, Abdikadir Mohamed (Ato), and Bill Jolitz.

Minnesotans can trace their families and their state's heritage to a multitude of ethnic groups. *The People of Minnesota* series tells each group's story in a compact, handsomely illustrated, and accessible paperback. Readers will learn about the group's accomplishments, ethnic organizations, settlement patterns, and occupations. Each book includes a personal story of one person or family, told through a diary, a letter, or an oral history.

Minnesota writer Bill Holm reminded us why these stories remain as important as ever: "To be ethnic, somehow, is to be human. Neither can we escape it, nor should we want to. You cannot interest yourself in the lives of your neighbors if you don't take sufficient interest in your own."

This series is based on the critically acclaimed book *They Chose Minnesota: A Survey of the State's Ethnic Groups* (Minnesota Historical Society Press). The volumes in *The People of Minnesota* bring each group's story up to date and add dozens of photographs to inform and enhance the telling.

Books in the series include *Swedes in Minnesota, Jews in Minnesota, Norwegians in Minnesota, African Americans in Minnesota,* and *Germans in Minnesota.*

About the Author

Ahmed Ismail Yusuf is a writer and an independent translator. His short stories in English have been published in *Bildhaan: An International Journal of Somali Studies* and *Mizna: Prose, Poetry and Art Exploring Arab America.* His work also appears in *Gororkii Yimi (The Vulture Has Landed),* a collection of short stories in Somali published by Ponte Invisible, Red Sea Online Publishing Group.